EXPERIENCES OF BEREA

The death of someone we love is a shocking and bewildering experience—probably the most stressful and devastating time of our lives.

Everyone's experience is unique. Yet through the sharing of reactions and feelings it is possible to find comfort and strength. The author, through years of hearing the stories and experience of bereaved people, and the insights of professionals, has compiled this book to share those experiences. Through reading how other people lived through their grief, readers may find strength in knowing they are not alone.

The work which has put author Helen Alexander in touch with all these people is, perhaps surprisingly, television. She has been in Religious Broadcasting with the BBC since 1981 and has, since 1990, been Editor of Worship Programmes for BBC Television, including *Songs of Praise*. She was producer of the series *Living with Dying*.

This book is for people who are still living with their own experience of bereavement, but it is also for anyone who wants to stand alongside people in grief. It is packed with people's experience and shared insights.

To Moreen and James, my parents, and
Rachael and Kathryn, my sisters.
Thank you for your love.

Experiences
of
Bereavement

Helen Alexander

A LION BOOK

Originally published as: *Bereavement: A Shared Experience*
Copyright © 1993 Helen Alexander
This edition published in 1997

The author asserts the moral right
to be identified as the author of this work

Published by
Lion Publishing plc
Sandy Lane West, Oxford, England
ISBN 0 7459 3753 5
Albatross Books Pty Ltd
PO Box 320, Sutherland, NSW 2232, Australia
ISBN 0 7324 1614 0

10 9 8 7 6 5 4 3 2 1 0

A catalogue record for this book is available
from the British Library

Printed and bound by Cox & Wyman, Reading, Great Britain

CONTENTS

INTRODUCTION

The death of someone we love will be one of the most stressful and devastating events of our lives. It is a shocking and bewildering experience and not something to be 'got over' in a matter of weeks or months. Grief is a long and individual process, and no two persons' experience is ever identical.

One thing that can help, however, is to share experiences with someone who has been through a similar ordeal. And that is what this book offers—detailed accounts of how other people felt, and came to live through their bereavement. The accounts are drawn together from many varying experiences, but the intensity of feeling expressed is the same. It is my hope that as you read how other people lived through their time of grief, and as they recount how they journeyed along a roller-coaster of emotions and questioning, you will draw strength and understanding for times when you feel similarly.

In this book I am drawing enormously on the wisdom and insight shared over the years by the people I've met, both those who have been bereaved and those who have a more professional interest—counsellors, clergy, doctors. I am not a bereavement counsellor, but in BBC Television's Worship Programmes where I work we receive letters almost daily from viewers who are struggling to make sense of pain and loss. Some of these people feel that God has deserted them; others feel that he is very close. Some viewers write of the death of partners several years previously and for these people the pain is still very real; others write of the death of a child and their sense of isolation when friends and neighbours cross the street to avoid talking to them.

Over the years I have come to realize how ill-equipped we are to deal with bereavement, both as a society and as a Christian community. I hope that this book, based on the experiences of others, offers a degree of insight and comfort to people who want to know how on earth other people learned to live with their bereavement.

Many people have helped shape the content of this book in all sorts of ways. I owe particular thanks to the Reverend Dr Anne Townsend, whose attentive reading of the text helped to firm up and sharpen what follows; the press office of SANDS; and those friends and colleagues who encouraged me to keep on writing!

London, Autumn 1992

1

'SO ALONE!'
The fact of death

I am devastated at losing my husband, who was my best friend as well. Words cannot describe the loneliness and desolation I feel. We had been married for fifty-two years, and I feel like I've lost a part of myself.

―――――――

I thought I was prepared for death, and for being on my own, but after thirty-five years of marriage I don't think you ever can be.

―――――――

When everyone had gone home after the funeral, I felt incredibly lost and sad. I didn't know what I should do next. I returned to work quite quickly but found I felt terribly tired and the tears welled up all too easily. I felt guilty, I felt empty.

―――――――

Death, no matter how it comes, whether expected or completely out of the blue, is an outrage. It can shake us to our very core and makes us question the purpose of life itself. Why are we born, if only to die? Why love, if it only results in pain? How can someone be here one minute and irrevocably gone the next?

Death makes us question the meaning of life itself. It also stirs up all kinds of strong and overwhelming emotions: anger at the person who has died; resentment at the apparent unfairness of it all—'Why me? I've never done anyone any harm'; guilt at all the things that happened over the years which resulted in arguments; or guilt again at taking that person for granted.

Yet death is inextricably a part of life. At an intellectual level we all know about death and say, wryly, 'Well, the one certain thing about life is death.' But at an emotional level, death appals us. It takes from us people who are part of our lives, and it removes from us people that we love. We might have faith that we will see them again, or we might believe that we will never see them again. Either way we don't know for sure. And in the meantime life goes on and somehow we've got to learn to live without the person or people whom death has stolen from us.

The process of adapting to profound feelings of loss, of dealing with an overwhelming sensation of grief, and of beginning to live again is known as bereavement. The Oxford Dictionary defines the verb bereave as 'rob, dispossess of, leave desolate', and these definitions aptly describe the responses felt by people who are coming to terms with the loss of someone they loved.

For people living in Britain in the 1990s bereavement has become a particularly difficult process. In a developed, techno-logical world, death itself has become a taboo subject. Advances in medical science along with a huge general improvement in nutrition, hygiene and living-standards have meant that, except through accident or rare illness, death has become a phenomenon of old age. It now represents failure for the medical profession and is something the rest of us prefer not to think about and quite successfully manage to avoid.

These, of course, are sweeping generalizations but society today is unused to dealing with death on a regular basis. Although it is such a natural part of life, it really has become the extraordinary part. Fatal accidents attract lurid headlines in local and sometimes national press: 'Mother of two dies in crash'. Death is also a convenient way of writing characters out of the ever-popular 'soaps' on television and radio. The knock-on effect seems to be that the only contact many people have with death, for long periods in their own lives, is by means of the media or through make-believe.

Rather than make us more sympathetic to people who are recently bereaved, these changes seem to have the opposite effect. Many of those who are newly bereaved talk of people literally crossing the road to avoid talking to them. Some recall being asked, four or six weeks later, 'Are you feeling better now?' They also say how much they need to talk about the person who has died, and yet how frequently that name is omitted from conversation.

Avoidance of talking about death (particularly our own) and confining it strictly to the world of drama or news headlines makes us ill-prepared to help the dying and the bereaved. When we also have to face the death of someone close to ourselves, we feel bewildered and confused.

Jane's story

Jane was thirty-two, and working full-time as a teacher at a local primary school. Her husband, John, was working long hours trying to build up his own business as a printer. For the past couple of years they had talked about starting a family but, with the rise in interest rates, the financial pressure on the business was great and they decided to wait until they were on a firmer financial footing. It was a Thursday evening, Jane recalls, when the phone rang. They had just finished a late meal and were sitting watching television.

I picked up the phone from where I sat in my chair. My father said, 'Jane' and then nothing else. He was breathing heavily and then began to cry. I remember shivering, and an icy flood of terror shot through my system. I was frightened of what he was trying to tell me. 'Dad, what is it? Tell me!' He then, all in a rush, told me that my mum had collapsed at home late that afternoon and that he'd returned from work to find her lying on the lounge floor. He'd called an ambulance, but she was dead by the time they got to the hospital.

I remember being unable to talk. John took over the phone, talked to my dad, and soon we were driving the two hundred miles to Birmingham to be with him. In one sense the days which followed are a complete blur but I remember thinking, as we drove up the motorway that night, that this wasn't real. It couldn't be happening to me. And yet one bit of me must have known it, because I felt like the rug had been pulled from under my feet and suddenly the world seemed like a very hostile place.

There are certain moments which still seem engrained in my memory. Suddenly, when I'm doing something mundane like the washing-up, or driving home from work, one of those moments will just appear from nowhere and take me completely by surprise. It's difficult to get rid of too, it's like I've got to keep going over and over it. One moment which keeps coming back is the day I started to go through my mother's things. I felt like an intruder working my way through the drawers of her dressing table. These were her intimate things, and they reminded me, oh, so painfully, that there was a side to my mother I never knew. And as I feel that, I feel the guilt too. The accusing inner voice that says, 'You shut your mother out, you didn't get to know her, you were too busy with your own life . . .' and so it goes on. I know too that she'd really have liked me to have had a baby, and I feel awful that I didn't have one because we'd decided we couldn't afford it yet!

My mother's death was six months ago now, but I still feel dreadful about it. I find it hard to believe she's really gone, and I keep thinking of things I want to tell her, things which I would never have talked to her about before. Suddenly, it's become important to me to have a child but John says we still can't afford to. I'm worried about my dad, too. I'm terrified something's going to happen to him. I keep phoning him up to ask how he's doing, and find that I want to be with him more than I did.

You know, I hear myself say all these things . . . I'm worried about this, terrified about that, guilty about the other, and I hardly recognize myself. I used to be so happy-go-lucky, but now Mum's died I suddenly feel very insecure. And although I'm married and John's being really supportive all the way through, in a funny way I feel quite lonely. My friends were all quite good to begin with, but it's like they think I should be over it by now. None of them has yet lost a parent and I think they find it uncomfortable to see how upset I still am.

Grief, as Jane indicates, is a very lonely experience. Each bereavement is unique. The range of feelings—from hurt to anger, from jealousy to guilt, and also from love to feeling let down and abandoned by the person who died when you still needed them—can only be experienced by you. Other family members are learning to live with their own loss, but only you know how you are feeling at any one particular time. Even then, it's possible that you cannot really identify what it is you are feeling. For your feelings may be confused and swing from one extreme to another.

People who are grieving can also experience a range of physical symptoms—insomnia, lack of appetite, headaches and tiredness. Couple these with sadness and waves of very unfamiliar and unpredictable feelings, and it is easy to see why this can be a very, very difficult time in anyone's life. Yet we are so unprepared for it, in ourselves or in other people.

Christian people in particular can find themselves thinking, if only I had more faith in God, then I wouldn't be feeling like this. Yet for people who have a very strong faith, the pain can be just as great. Sometimes it can be worse.

Malcolm's story

Malcolm had been married to Julia for forty years. They led a normal life in a very normal suburban estate and in the course of their marriage they had faced very few ups and downs. One of their sadnesses was that they had never been able to have children, but that fact had brought them closer together and their marriage was a strong one.

It was only a month after Malcolm's retirement when Julia was diagnosed as having advanced lung cancer and the doctors announced that there was nothing further they could do. Throughout their married life Julia and Malcolm had attended church regularly and were regarded as stalwart members of their local Methodist church. In the three months before her death Julia found more and more comfort in her faith; and the friendships she had formed at the church brought much support as people there flocked to help. Malcolm, though, felt his heart hardening. In prayer he pleaded with God to let Julia live, and when well-meaning friends spoke of God's mercy in allowing Julia a quick and dignified death, he felt an anger that he would never have suspected he was capable of.

Julia's death was dignified; her pain was well controlled and she received very good nursing care at home. At her funeral service the church was packed, and the congregation sang the hymns she had chosen, lustily and with gratitude for Julia's friendship. The minister spoke of Julia's calm and accepting faith, and of his certainty that she now was in a better place where she would know no more pain. Malcolm picks up the story from there.

I sat there in the church feeling cold and hard. I couldn't cry, but I felt overpowering anger. How could they be so cheerful about Julia's death, how dare they praise God for taking her away from me? All my life I had faithfully attended church, all my life I had believed in a God of love who heard us in our distress. Now I was doubting if any of it was really true. And if it wasn't all a sham, and there really was a God, why had he not heard my prayers and let Julia live some more? I needed her.

The next few weeks I hid myself away at home. I didn't want to see anyone, I certainly didn't want to talk. At first the people who had popped in and out of the house while Julia was ill, came round. But because I was so taciturn and distant they soon stopped coming. The minister called a couple of times too but I was too ashamed to say that I now questioned whether or not there really was a God. So we just had a really stilted conversation which I suspect both of us found profoundly uncomfortable.

During this time I really let myself go. I didn't eat properly and I started to drink quite heavily. It was the only way I could get through the evening. The alcohol was the anaesthetic that took my pain away because the loneliness I felt was unbearable.

I also couldn't quite believe deep down that Julia really had died. If I heard a noise I'd think it was Julia—coming in from shopping or tidying things up in the bedroom, and then a split second later I'd have to tell myself again that no, it wasn't, Julia was dead.

I didn't wash my clothes, I did no housework and in my deepest moments of despair I'd find myself calling out to God aloud, shouting, 'Why did you take her?' Sometimes I'd whisper, 'Come on God, if you're really there, show me, give me the proof!' Julia had abandoned me by dying and God had abandoned me too.

Then one afternoon, about two months after Julia's death, I just felt this tremendous surge of anger—at Julia for dying; at God for not being there; at our so-called friends who had so quickly disappeared off the scene. I found myself picking up a table lamp made from heavy glass and hurling it with all of my strength through the lounge window. It was like I'd a desperate need to smash or destroy which had been bottled up so long that now it was just erupting like a volcano. And then the tears came, virtually the first tears I had shed since she died, and I cried. How I cried! Great heaving sobs which just went on and on.

I've no idea how much time passed but suddenly I became aware that there was a policewoman in the room. She was incredibly kind, explaining that the neighbours alerted them because they had heard the sound of breaking glass. She went and made us both a cup of tea and then sat with me, encouraging me to talk, and out it all came—all the stuff I've just told you, and lots more besides. Eventually, she said she had to go, but would I mind if she contacted a social worker. I wanted to say no, but by then I realized I probably needed some help to get sorted out and so agreed.

That was all three years ago now and I really thank God for that policewoman. I only ever saw her that day, but through the social worker I went along to some kind of bereavement club. Everyone who went had lost somebody close to them and when we met we talked about how we were faring. It sounds morbid, but through that group I realized that I wasn't going crazy—even though you do feel like you're going mad—and that other people felt like I did.

I still have my down moments, don't get me wrong, but gradually I've got myself together again. I'm not the same as I was before Julia's death, I never will be. But in a funny sort of way I'm stronger. Julia was always there for me, all the way through our married life, so I've had to learn to live on my own. I'm ashamed to say I've even had to learn to cook. I'm quite good at it now!

And my faith? It's back, quieter maybe, but much deeper. I realize God was there, all the way through. As the saying goes, if the sun is hidden by clouds it doesn't mean that it isn't there. I was so caught up in all that I was feeling I just couldn't allow God to get close. But what I've also realized is that it was all right to get angry with God; maybe it's one of the few times I've truly been honest with God. I've always subjected him to my 'Sunday-best' behaviour before, but now he's got me as I really am. God could cope with my anger. He wasn't going to break just because I prayed in a few choice swear-words.

I don't go to the old church any more, though, because they couldn't bear to share the pain I was feeling. It was all about what I ought to be thinking and feeling, and what I've realized now is that grief comes in all shapes and sizes and that God's prepared to take all of it, just as it comes.

So now I go along to the church just round the corner. It's ever so small and the congregation is only about thirty on a normal Sunday, but it seems right somehow. I cut the grass for them and handle the accounts, and it seems like there's a place for me there.

I still miss Julia, though. There's still not a day goes past and I haven't thought of her at least once. But I've got some happy memories of our years together and I really believe that one day we'll be together again.

Malcolm's story is a typical one and indicates just how long a journey grief and learning to live with it can be. It also shows that grief can make us behave in ways that can take us by surprise and which we can find disturbing, even shaming. Losing someone we love to the finality of death turns our lives upside down. A void of longing and needing is opened up and it takes time to adjust to that void. Through it all the important thing to remember is that whether we have a very strong faith, or none at all, or whether we are somewhere in the middle, there will be a void. God is not a replacement for human love. When we have lost someone who was a part of our life, someone who loved us and who we loved in return, someone who cuddled us and held us and made us laugh, then we have a human right to miss them.

Even if that person had endured a poor quality of life and even if it came as a relief that the suffering ended, we will still mourn. We mourn for the very simple reason that a person we loved is no longer with us. And the right to mourn is one that nobody should try and take away from us and which we all need to learn to respect.

Obviously, there are degrees of justice in loss. The death of someone aged ninety, after a full and active life, has a sense of rightness about it. The death of a child of six, mown down by a drunken driver, seems futile and outrageous. Both people will be mourned by those close to them, but while the first death can be accepted as 'natural', the second will provoke such anger and bitterness that it will be very difficult indeed for the rest of the family. Parents, grandparents, brothers and sisters, will have a long way to travel before they feel that they have picked up the pieces of their lives again. In some cases marriages split, so destructive is the grief felt by one or both parents.

So where is God in all of this? Is God in it at all? Faith says that God is there at the very heart of the worst of our grieving. God weeps with those who weep and yet also wipes away every tear, so the scriptures tell us. It is a reassuring and comforting image. But humanity, intellect, ask just how is God a part of all this? The words sound fine, the concept is desirable, but how do we know it's true?

Does it just boil down to faith after all? Or are there other ways, perhaps seen in the experiences of others, which point to God being an integral part of the lonely, aching, grieving process?

Jennifer's story

Jennifer had just turned thirty when her life was turned horribly upside down. Two days into a family holiday at a popular Mediterranean resort, all had seemed right with the world. Jennifer had lain back on the warm sand, feeling herself beginning to relax for the first time since her divorce had become final just three weeks before. Her two daughters, Emma aged eight and Rosemary aged six, were playing at the water's edge down on the beach. They were amusing themselves quite happily and seemed content to obey her instruction not to wander away on their own.

Jennifer nodded off into a light sleep and then, suddenly, found herself waking up, pangs of fear tying her stomach in knots. Where were the girls? They weren't at the water's edge any more. Terrified, not understanding where the fear was coming from but nonetheless sensing that something was terribly wrong, she began to run the length of the beach to where a crowd of people had gathered at the bottom of a cliff. The drone of a helicopter got closer and sirens were sounding in the distance. Then she saw Emma, distraught, clutching a stranger's hand; and just a few yards away, at the bottom of the cliff, lay Rosemary's spread-eagled body, her head at an odd angle. Her younger daughter was dead, her neck broken, after a twenty-foot fall.

Four years on Jennifer shudders at the memory, remembering the struggle to retain her sanity.

I was a Christian before Rosemary died, although I sensed that some people at church thought a true Christian shouldn't have got divorced. But my faith was strong, and I had a real sense that although my marriage had ended in failure, God was going to use that somehow in his plans for my life.

So when Rosemary was killed by such a freak accident I felt appalled. Perhaps I'd got it all wrong, and the God of love was really someone cold who punished people who broke his laws. Was Rosemary's death a punishment for my divorce? I just couldn't get the thought out of my head. It tormented me.

Friends arranged for me to spend a week in retreat with a contemplative order of nuns. As their chanted prayers echoed around the old chapel, I sensed that God was very close. There was a tangible presence of something which felt holy and special, but welcoming. There was an enormous realization that this was no 'punishing' presence, but a loving one, just as I'd been taught and just as I had once believed. The tears poured down my face as with gratitude I praised God for his goodness.

How could I do it? My heart was still breaking with the loss of my daughter and that pain was still there, but I was able to see that God hadn't caused Rosemary to try and climb that cliff. Also, when I wondered why he hadn't eased her fall, I had to remember that he had not intervened when Jesus cried in agony from the cross, 'My God, my God, why have you forsaken me?' I sensed that there was a kind of natural law, or a God-given law if you prefer. And this law has us born into this life (and as infants in the womb we have no knowledge as to what lies ahead); and when we die, whether young or old, we are born into the next world. Death is the mechanism that takes our spirits on,

*like butterflies emerging from the chrysalis. I'm not saying that I
believe God wanted Rosemary and so caused her to fall, but her
premature death, so awful by our standards, has ushered Rosemary
into his presence and with him she's in very safe hands.*

*I have to believe this, because if there is no 'next world' or heaven
then Rosemary's short life meant nothing. She was a random collection
of cells that ceased to exist. Life just has to be more than that! Emma
often talks about her sister, sometimes she talks to her. I wasn't sure
this was very healthy, but my vicar said to let her be. Emma just says
that she likes talking to her sister. She's not sure that Rosemary hears
her, but likes to think that she might!*

Jennifer's account of how she was able to see God through the
death of her daughter is a remarkable one. How right she is to
look to the place of birth, life and death, in an attempt to
understand a tragic accident. If we can really see that death is
the means to 'another phase', then it does lend value and
meaning to this life. It certainly won't take the pain of grief
away, but it adds meaning where otherwise there would be
nothing but a sense of futility. It will still feel unfair, and
Jennifer is the first to say that she still asks, 'Why me? First a
divorce and then my child's death!' But her faith gives a
perspective that helps her to make sense of it all.

But what of my question which demanded to know if God
really is at the heart of our grief, sharing it? While he is welcoming
another of his children into a new existence, does he also
recognize that those left behind are paying the price of human
loving? Jennifer was helped by recalling Jesus on the cross, when
he knew of the life to come but also felt the agony of being
abandoned. The nearest I can get to an answer is to turn to St
John's account of the death of Lazarus, the brother of Martha and
Mary.

The story of Lazarus is a powerful one. In Chapter 11 of John's
Gospel, we read that Jesus loved Mary, Martha and Lazarus but
that, on hearing of Lazarus' illness, he waited two days before
heading off to Bethany—possibly because it was a dangerous
place for him to go. Interestingly, Thomas is reported as saying to
the other disciples that they should go along too, and die as well!

By the time they got to Bethany, however, it transpired that Lazarus had already been dead for four days. Many people were there consoling the sisters as was the Jewish custom of the day, but when Jesus arrived both Martha and Mary rebuked him, asserting that if only he'd been present he would have prevented Lazarus from dying. Mary was weeping, as were many of the other mourners, and Jesus (already having predicted that he would 'wake Lazarus from sleep') wept too, being 'deeply moved in spirit and troubled' (John 11:33–35).

It's interesting to note that although the Revised Standard Version of the Bible says Jesus is 'deeply moved', the original Greek implies a sense of anger. Biblical commentators speculate as to why Jesus should feel such anger. Perhaps it was because his beloved friends were having to undergo such an ordeal? Certainly as we think about bereavement it's important to know that Jesus himself knew grief and frustration, both at the loss of a friend and at the pain Lazarus' sisters felt as they mourned their brother.

Jesus then went on to raise Lazarus from the dead and that is usually the focus of this particular story. But I want to stop before this to emphasize that, even though Jesus knew Lazarus would live again, he was still troubled so much by the weeping and distress of others that he, too, wept. In this account I believe we catch a glimpse of how God weeps with us in our grief, while at the same time knowing the reason for each death and having a greater purpose. The God who weeps with us and who shares our anger is also a God who is neither powerless nor impotent. Out of this terrible thing can come re-creation and renewal.

In subsequent chapters I hope we will be exploring some of the really big questions that death poses: What is the purpose of life? What is death? How do we come to learn more of the nature of God through all of this?

However, I also hope that we will explore practical, down-to-earth issues. The experiences of others who have lived through bereavement may be particularly valuable here, and perhaps they can show us—as a society and as individuals—how much better we could help those who grieve.

SO ALONE!

☐ Death is an outrage. Intellectually we may try to fool ourselves that death is merely part of the life cycle, but when it comes close it is shocking. We don't expect death, and its irrevocability can be terrifying.

☐ Bereavement is a long process. We do not recover from it in days or weeks, as if we'd just had a bad dose of flu. We need a long time to adjust to losing someone who was a major part of our lives.

☐ Grief unlocks all manner of strong feelings. It is common for people to think they might be going slightly mad, but bewildering feelings of all sorts are perfectly normal. Another common feeling and one which surprises people is anger. It may be anger at the loved one for daring to die, or even at something seemingly trivial like not having cut the grass before 'going out and getting killed'!

☐ No matter how strong our faith, we are still allowed to feel bereft. To lose someone we love leaves a void and it is right that we are able to acknowledge that loss. In so many ways it's the price we pay for the gift of human love.

☐ Death is a natural part of life. It permits our spirit to move on to whatever lies beyond death.

☐ God shares our grief. In the depth of the pain and the loss and the anger and the confusion, God is right there with us.

2

SAYING GOODBYE
Acknowledging reality

Once I knew that Matthew was dead I asked the casualty staff if I could see him. I'm glad that I did, because I could then see that he really was dead, and that rather than looking grotesque, he looked peaceful.

I talked with Dad about his funeral service about two weeks before he died. He chose two readings, and the hymns, and made it clear that he wanted a service in the church to which everyone who knew him was welcome to come. He didn't want any floral tributes, but for the money to go to one of the cancer charities. It was a good service and I was glad that he had planned it.

The service at the crematorium was awful! We had to wait outside for the previous service to finish, and then the vicar (who none of us knew) kept calling my aunt Georgina, but we'd always known her as Jane. She hated being called Georgina, said it made her feel like she was a naughty girl at school! And then for the hymns we were singing along to a tape. Ghastly!

One of the effects of death being such a taboo subject these days is that, apart from of those who come across it in the course of their work (the emergency services, health professionals, ministers and funeral directors), most of us meet death only through the images we see on television or in newspapers. Many people will say that they have never seen the body of someone who has died.

Today, though, the considered wisdom of psychologists and of people who work in bereavement counselling is that being able to see the body of someone who has died is a good step towards accepting that the person really has died. Even if the death was the result of a road traffic accident or some other such horrific event, it is still possible to spend time with the body. If staff feel the injuries are so great that it would be less distressing not to see the body, it is feasible just to sit beside the covered body, perhaps holding the hand, or a ring.

This kind of contact is recommended because the human mind is complex and sometimes confusing. When traumatic events happen to us, we subconsciously, and even consciously, find ways to deny them, particularly if it is something we did not witness with our own eyes. Unless we are able to see that something really has happened then a part of us will behave as if it hasn't. We must try to face up to the reality of the trauma, painful as that can be. Only then will we begin to find ways of dealing with it.

Death has indeed become so alien to our everyday experience, so much something that we dread (if we're truly honest with ourselves), that it is very difficult to take in—especially if we were not there at the time it happened. But even if we were there, and know with our heads that someone has died, the heart can lag behind. The cords of love which knit our relationships with people we're close to are not severed by death. By taking time to be with the person who has just died, there's an opportunity for the heart to catch up. And as the reality sinks in, it becomes possible to begin to say goodbye.

Pauline's story

Pauline and her husband, David, had been married for sixteen years, and had children aged fourteen, eleven and three. One evening David found that he had run out of his favourite

23

tobacco. The corner shop two streets away would still be open, so he decided to walk round to buy some. It was a pleasant evening and Pauline decided to go with him. The three-year old was already asleep in bed and the other two were busy doing homework, so she saw no harm in leaving the house.

As they crossed the road at the pelican crossing, a transit van stopped to let them cross. But a car in the outside lane, failing to see the red light at the pelican crossing accelerated past the transit van and hit David as he was crossing the road. His body was carried some distance by the car and then fell back on the road as the car driver slowed.

Pauline raced to him as did a nurse who was walking by. 'Don't move him!' she said as Pauline went to cradle his head. The nurse felt for David's pulse. 'He's still alive!' she said, 'But he's very badly injured.' After what felt like an age but was only a matter of minutes, the police and an ambulance appeared. Pauline went in the ambulance with David, numbly watching.

I sat there, willing him to live. I'll never forget that journey as long as I live. I kept praying that David would just open his eyes, but he never did. And I just shook. My hands and legs wouldn't stop trembling, and the whole time I watched as the ambulance man worked on David.

Then we raced up to the hospital with the sirens blaring, and the doors were flung open. Now I realize that my last glimpse of David alive was of him being taken away from me by a whole posse of white coats and uniforms. A nurse stopped me from following and ushered me into a waiting room. I don't know how long I sat there. All I remember is willing David to live. A policewoman came wanting details of what had happened. I can't remember if it was her or the nurse who phoned my friend Anne to ask her to look after the children. Then a doctor came and said that David needed to go to theatre because he had severe bleeding in his brain and they had to relieve the pressure as soon as possible.

I just couldn't believe this was happening to me. It was all a dream. Soon, I must wake up. Ten o'clock. Just three hours since we'd decided to go for a walk. The door opened and time stood still. I'll never ever forget the look on the doctor's face. She put a hand on my shoulder and said, 'I'm terribly sorry, but your husband died just a few minutes ago. He had extensive injuries which, in time, he had might have recovered from, but the damage to the brain was too great.'

I felt a pain through me that pierced me to the chair. No, not David, not us. What had we done to hurt anyone? We didn't deserve this. And then I began to laugh, hysterically. All of this had happened because David wanted some tobacco. It was absurd. Who'd heard of anyone literally *dying for a smoke!*

And then the crying started. Deep, deep sobbing but then, more than anything else, I realized I desperately wanted to see David and heard myself asking if I could see him. Funnily enough, I didn't think they'd let me but they said I could. Then I got frightened, fearful of what he'd be like. I'm incredibly squeamish, but yet I felt really strongly that I wanted to go to him. He was my husband, and these white coats had whisked him away from me. I had to see him.

And I did, in a small room off the mortuary. There was a chaplain there because someone had asked if I wanted one. He was very kind and asked me if I'd like him to pray. I wanted that. I wanted to hear that David was committed into God's safe keeping; and then he encouraged me to sit with David. I think the chaplain then went and sat quietly outside but all I remember is sitting beside David, stroking his face and, from time to time, kissing him. His head was covered in a bandage and there was a huge lump on his cheek, but otherwise he looked like he did when he was asleep.

I talked to him, told him how much I loved him, asked him how on earth he thought I was going to manage without him. And then I got angry with him, furious that it was his wish to carry on smoking that had got us into this mess. Through it all, though, I kept expecting him to jump up and say, 'Had you fooled there, didn't I?' Except, of course, he never did.

I went back to see him the next day too. There was going to be a post-mortem and in a strange way I welcomed that because it would show why he had died; but this time I went back with the children. I hadn't really wanted them to come but the two eldest ones had asked. I thought it would frighten them, but the chaplain had said it might help them. He stressed that the children should be given the choice, but in no way should they feel forced one way or the other.

Anne kept the youngest outside while I went in with the other two.

Jim, the eleven-year old, touched his dad and said how cold he felt. I was surprised how different David looked now, compared to last night. His skin was almost waxy, and I had an overwhelming sense that this was the body David had left behind. The night before David looked just as if he was asleep, but now it was like it was David, but it wasn't, all at the same time. What I'd begun to realize was that this body and all that had gone to make David as he was, were two separate things.

Obviously we were all really upset, but we were able to cry together. We cuddled one another a lot, not talking very much and then the boys left and Anne brought Janie in. She kept saying, 'I want my daddy' and so I took her over saying, 'Daddy's died, Janie. He's gone to heaven to live with Jesus.' And do you know what she said? It was the very question I was asking, 'Why?'

How do you answer a question you don't know the answer to? All I could say was, 'Janie, I don't know why Jesus wants Daddy now. We all want him here; but Jesus will take really good care of him.'

Afterwards I discovered that David's family were horrified that I'd taken the children in to see him, particularly Janie. But what's the best thing to do? Tell her her daddy has died and let her see him, lying peacefully and not covered in blood? Or just say that he's gone away, he couldn't say goodbye and that she will never see him again? I'm convinced I did the right thing for her.

About two years after David's death I asked the boys if I'd been wrong in letting them see their father's body, but they were adamant it was OK. Jim even said he'd had this awful picture in his mind of how his dad must look after being run over, and that it was a relief to see how he looked. He said he'd kept having awful pictures in his mind but seeing how peaceful his dad looked the pictures had gone away.

I know that for me it was essential to see David's body several times. It was like I had to keep going back to check that he really was dead. I'd dreaded seeing him after the post-mortem but he looked all right and at least I knew that no one could have saved him. The bleeding in his brain had been so great that too much damage had been done.

By the time it came to the funeral service at the crematorium I think I had accepted that David was dead. Certainly when the coffin slid away from view and I knew his body would be burned by the end of the day, I knew it was David's body and not David himself that would be incinerated. That helped me enormously, otherwise I don't think I could ever have let them cremate David. I loved him so much but what was left was a shell that he no longer needed. Don't ask me where he was. I'm not sure I believe in a life after death, but I knew that what went to make David into the man I'd gladly have died for wasn't in that body any more.

The journey to acceptance which the path of bereavement represents is a long and difficult process of learning to say goodbye. Goodbye means letting go. It is a separation marked by sadness, yes; but it is a realization that things are now different.

On a more general level I've always hated goodbyes. Many a sodden tissue has marked my taking leave of people I'm close to—not because they have died, I hasten to add, but just because I'm saying goodbye and there is five hundred miles between us.

But perhaps there is a parallel. Thinking about why some of my own departures are so tearful it's that, apart from being a sentimental softie at heart, I'm also recognizing the separation from people I love—even if I'm not very good at telling them so.

That is why bereavement is also about saying goodbye. Death is the great separator. It pushes someone we love from this world into whatever lies beyond and as the people left behind we have to learn to live with that separation. Saying goodbye is the way we ackowledge that the person we love has gone; and the first stage is to allow ourselves to feel that loss.

That's so much easier to say than to do. There are so many things to be done at the time of a death that it is possible to allow busyness to keep the feelings at bay. It's probably particularly difficult for men to allow themselves to express their loss. Whereas most women feel able to cry in public, most men do not.

In this chapter the 'saying goodbye' takes two forms. Firstly, it involves beginning to recognize the reality of the situation: death really has happened. Secondly, it means formalizing that goodbye in a time-worn ritual, the funeral. There are, of course, a number of other ways in which people make their goodbyes over a period of time, but they are on a longer time-scale and are dealt with in the other chapters.

Seeing the body, in death, is one way of recognizing the reality of what has happened. If the death occurs in hospital, most staff today understand that an opportunity to see the body can be beneficial. Equally, there is an acceptance that people should not feel forced to do it. It should be an individual decision.

In Pauline's case it was instinct that drove her to ask to see her husband's body, but what happens if there is no body or the body is so severely damaged that it really would cause distress?

Alex's story

Alex's wife, Louise, died at the age of forty while abroad on a business trip to Hong Kong.

I never ever saw her body. She was cremated out there and we just had a very simple ceremony back here when we scattered the ashes. I was quite calm through it all, very businesslike, and was back at work within a week. Colleagues kept saying things like, 'You're so brave', and I was pleased that they thought I was coping so well. But a few days later Louise's suitcase, with all her belongings, was returned to me. That did it. I just broke down and sobbed. I realized that, in some way, I'd still been expecting her to return, and now here was the first proof that she wouldn't. I think that's when I really started to grieve for her.

Denial is a very common human protective mechanism. It happens in the case of serious illness when, to begin with, the symptoms are ignored in the hope that they will go away. When they don't go away and the doctors begin to suggest that something serious could be going on, patients will often say, 'I'm sure they're making a fuss about nothing,' or their friends and relatives will say, 'It'll be fine, you'll see!' And when it is established that serious illness is indeed present it is common to think that the doctors have made a mistake, or muddled up the results with someone else's.

Later on, of course, it can work the other way. Many people with a terminal illness intuitively know that they are dying and yet feel forced to go on with the denial that others are living out around them.

It's easy to see why we do it, too. Who wants to face up to the fact that we, or someone we love, might have cancer or any other life-threatening illness? Who wants to be reminded of the reality of what it means to be mortal? These are tragedies that befall other people, not us.

That is why one of the commonest first reactions in bereavement is disbelief. Protecting ourselves from our own mortality, and that of people we love (probably quite rightly, because to live daily with such intensity of feeling is more than a person can bear), it is difficult to take in that it really has happened to us. That is why many people find that seeing the body of the person who has died is the first step in absorbing the truth of what has happened.

That was certainly Pauline's reaction when she spoke of her husband David's death. She said that it helped her separate David and all that she knew of him from the inert, battered body he had left behind. This seems to be a very common reaction. Whether or not they are religious, people often talk of sensing that the person they loved has left the body. They even say the body seems like an empty shell.

This in turn can help the process of saying goodbye, or letting go. Think for the moment of the point in the funeral service where the coffin is either lowered into the ground, or disappears towards the furnaces in the crematorium. It can be extremely distressing to think that the person we loved so dearly is about to be buried, or burned. Yet, being able to separate the body from the spirit means that when the coffin disappears from view it is not the person as we knew them who is being buried, but the body they have no further need of. If there hasn't been some progress towards acceptance that the person really is dead then, in a terrible way, there is a sense in which we might feel they are being buried or burned alive. Not rationally, of course, but who is rational at a time like that?

The second part of saying goodbye, in the early days, is through the age-old ritual of the funeral. From the beginning of the human race it seems that there has always been some kind of ceremony marking the death of an individual. Egyptian pharaohs were buried with a collection of objects they might find useful in the afterlife—drinking vessels, weapons, jewellery. Many societies set aside a ritual time of mourning, recognizing the need for grieving people to be given time to come to terms with their loss.

How on earth did a part of British society ever get to the awful situation where twenty minutes at the crematorium with a few sandwiches and a drink afterwards were all that were really required to mark someone's life and death? It cheapens life, and it denies the strength of human feeling and emotion. It might feel more comfortable to find ways of avoiding the pain which death brings, no matter how expected and timely the event, but it devalues the gift and meaning of life itself.

Of course this kind of experience is not the only one found in the United Kingdom. The rousing send-off represented by the wake can still be found; and there are other religious and cultural traditions in this country where the emphasis is not only on supporting the people who are grieving, but also on celebrating the life that has just passed.

Funerals are one way of valuing the life of the person who died and it is possible to add personal touches which, later on, offer a good memory. Of course, not everyone will want to do this, feeling that the words already given are all that they can take, but some people do become involved in the planning, and are glad to do so.

Oliver and Naomi's story

Oliver and Naomi's life fell apart after their four year old son, Paul, was diagnosed as having a rare and untreatable form of cancer. He was ill for just two months. Most of that time was spent in hospital and Naomi virtually lived there so that she could be with Paul through it all. She helped in his nursing, and the staff on the ward became her friends. They were fond of Paul, as they were of all the children they nursed, but he was there for a comparatively long time and they got know him, learning how to win him over and engage his co-operation. During this time Oliver had continued working, and although he visited at weekends and during the evenings, he began to feel left out.

There didn't seem to be anything he could do for Paul, Naomi and the staff were doing that. He was just the breadwinner who turned up, bearing gifts of new toys or sweets.

With Naomi sleeping over at the hospital and spending such a short time at home, Oliver regretted that they had so little time together. Nor was there anyone could talk to about it. His business colleagues were solicitous but anxious to avoid upsetting him by probing too deeply, and nearly all the people he knew in the village were really Naomi's friends.

It became apparent that Paul had very little time left. He had slipped into unconsciousness and so Oliver took leave from work to join the vigil at Paul's bedside. Together he and Naomi sat there, holding Paul's hand, stroking his hair that had only just begun to grow again after the chemotherapy. They talked to him from time to time, cuddling him, holding him, but knew he could probably no longer hear. Occasionally they talked briefly to one another, mostly asking if the other was OK, yet aware that together they were holding a vigil of love as they watched their young son's life slip away.

From time to time members of the nursing and medical staff came to check on Paul, but everyone knew there was nothing further they could do. Now they cared for Oliver and Naomi, encouraging them to drink a little of this, nibble a bit of that. Staff who'd become friends over the last weeks weren't afraid to show their own sadness and reached out to Oliver and Naomi, offering what little comfort they could. A hug here, a pat of the hand there.

The chaplain came too. She offered prayers for Paul and his parents and sat quietly with them until she was called away to meet the parents of a dangerously ill baby.

Paul died at six that evening, very peacefully.

By eight, Oliver and Naomi were back in their home together. Naomi was tired and drained in a way Oliver had never seen before and he encouraged her to take just one of the tranquillizers prescribed sparingly by a doctor at the hospital. Then with Naomi in bed asleep, Oliver began the task of phoning around relatives and close friends to tell them that Paul had just died.

I t choked me to do it, but I realized that here was something I could do. During so much of Paul's illness I had felt powerless. There had been so little I could do for him, but now, though it was a grim role, there was something I could do. Naomi was completely spent, not surprisingly, so it was down to me.

When I phoned the local vicar, who had been very good to us through Paul's illness, he asked if I would like to talk about the funeral service. I couldn't think what there was to discuss. I thought it was dust to dust, ashes to ashes, and all the other words the prayer books carry. He said that of course there were the words, but maybe there might be other things we'd like to do? Suddenly I wanted to know more and asked if he could come over there and then.

And he did, even though it was quite late by then. Over a glass of whisky each, he went through the service with me, and then asked me to think about readings we might like. Were there particular hymns, maybe ones that Paul had enjoyed? Were there people who might like to read or lead the prayers? Suddenly I was off. What was that chorus Paul would not stop singing when he came back from Sunday school?

The vicar left, leaving me with a list of readings from the Bible that we might like to look at, saying he'd be in touch the next day. I sat down then with the Bible and for the first time since my grandmother had given it to me, opened it, and worked my way through the readings. It was a bit tricky to find them but at least there was an index!

I sat there reading way past midnight. The words meant something in a way I'd never noticed before. God wasn't really a part of my life, and church was something I thought of as a place for women and children. But in the silence of that house, where Paul's voice would never be heard again, I began to wonder.

Paul had died on a Thursday, and his funeral was the next Monday. Naomi, too, liked the idea of making Paul's service special and so on Friday morning we began to plan. In an odd sort of way we enjoyed it. It was like it was the one last thing we could do for Paul, and something we could do together.

What did we do? Well, we threw it open to the entire village. A child's death is a dreadful thing and we wanted anyone to come along to the service who wanted to, children as well. And we invited the staff on the ward, and my colleagues from work, as well as relatives, of course.

The Sunday school children had made an altar frontal which had

'Goodbye Paul' on it; the senior registrar who had tried so hard to save Paul read 2 Corinthians 1:3–5; and I read that passage from Revelation 21 about the new heaven and the new earth. I wasn't sure I would be able to get through it, but I did. The last words were, 'He who conquers shall have this heritage, and I will be his God and he will be my son.' That had said so much to Naomi and I when we had been trying to find readings and we both agreed I should try to do it myself.

And the hymns? Well, the packed church all stood and sang, 'Jesus bids us shine with a pure clear light', which was the chorus Paul had sung over and over again when he first learned it; and one of the nurses from the hospital who has a beautiful voice had asked if she might sing at the service. We were delighted that she'd asked, and she sang 'Pie Jesus' from the Fauré Requiem.

I suspect everyone in the church was in tears at some point during the service, but that's OK. It was a service for Paul and the beauty was that it felt like it. One of my colleagues said to me, a few months afterwards, that he had enjoyed Paul's funeral. And I knew exactly what he meant!

What was good about the day was that Naomi and I felt so supported by the people there—the villagers, the hospital staff, our friends and relatives. And now you're going to think we really did go over the top, but we had some photos taken that day. The vicar said he didn't mind if that was what we wanted, and so we had just a few taken. We've got them in an album now. On the front it very simply says 'Paul' and we've put in there the pictures we believe tell the story of Paul's short life. It begins with the ultrasound scan picture when he was still a baby in the womb, has pictures taken at his birth, his birthdays and holidays, and it ends with the funeral pictures, the very last one of which is the altar frontal saying 'Goodbye Paul'.

We treasure that photo album. It's three years now since Paul died and we don't look at it as much as we did in the early days, but on the date of his birthday or the anniversary of his death, we will always spend time looking at it, remembering. And we've another child now, Emma, who's only six months old. But when she's old enough we'll tell her about Paul and let her meet in a very small way the memory of the brother she never knew.

When I tell people about Paul's funeral they often ask me how I felt *through it. Wasn't it all just too indescribably painful? But because Naomi and I were so well supported by the village, and because everyone was sharing our grief that day, in some strange way it was therapeutic. I cried, especially when I saw the altar frontal that the Sunday school children had made. But the service was there to mark Paul's short life and it did that. Perhaps if Paul had died suddenly then I might have felt differently, but we had a bit of time to adjust and our grieving began the day we were told he was terminally ill.*

Oliver's moving account of Paul's funeral shows how the day can be a good memory. Not everyone will feel that in similar circumstances they could have done the same thing. But it doesn't take too much emotional strength to think of music or readings, if the person who died hasn't already made their wishes known.

If you don't know the clergy in the area where a funeral will be held, and yet you would like the service to be personal, a good funeral director will be able to guide you. Clergy, like all other people, have strong points and weak points and you may feel easier with some than others. Moreover, it is clear from talking to funeral directors and the staff at crematoria that you can choose from a vast array of service styles. There is everything from the formal occasion where no one really knew the deceased and just wants to do the right thing, to colourful, emotional and lengthy services which include the occasional jazz or pipe band.

Saying goodbye is the first stage of beginning to live through grief. It means being able to acknowledge that someone really has died. It may well involve seeing the body and it will certainly involve a funeral ceremony of some sort. Many people, I suspect, see the funeral service as something of an ordeal. Not because of its religious and spiritual content, but because on the whole it is a peculiarly British (perhaps just English) habit to be fearful of public emotion—a great desire not to be seen crying in public.

Yet grief is about loss, loss of someone we loved or who was a part of our lives. I remember hearing an account of a West Indian funeral, where a young man had been fatally stabbed. From the moment it was known he had died the house was full of people who came to express sorrow and sympathy. His friends came by and talked at length about him, telling sometimes hilarious stories about what he'd said and done. The service in the church lasted for over two hours. There was much singing and much crying, and grief was expressed loudly and dramatically. The committal at the graveyard was no less emotional; and some of the white people who had attended the funeral, never having been to a West Indian service before, were amazed at how much of the pain and tragedy was expressed. They couldn't help but compare it to the carefully controlled, short, English service they had been to recently.

The expression of grief is partly a cultural thing, of course, and people need to be able to express their grief in the ways they want to. I suppose all I feel is that if we try to control the pain we feel, we don't always honour the life and memory of the person who died. Death is the taboo subject of the late twentieth century, but that taboo should not take away our right, and need, to grieve.

SAYING GOODBYE

☐ Seeing is believing. Bereavement can begin with a gap between our heads and our hearts. Intellectually we know that a death has occurred, but our hearts cannot accept it. Seeing the body of the person who died can be a help in beginning to acknowledge the loss.

☐ Don't exclude children. Even very young children are able to be included. They too know something is wrong and, if they are excluded, they feel that in some way the loss of the person is somehow their fault. They are confronted by much violent death on the television screens: give them a chance to see that it can be peaceful.

☐ Think about what will make the funeral a good memory for you and your family. It is a chance to say goodbye publicly, as well as to commit your loved one to God's care. It doesn't take long to give the service something of the uniqueness of the life you are now mourning.

3

'IT'S LIKE MY HEART IS BREAKING!'

The truth sinks in

Before Richard's funeral I was very busy. Making arrangements, phoning friends and, would you believe, tidying the house? But then afterwards, it hit me. An awful realization that Richard was dead. He wasn't going to walk through the door, grinning, saying, 'Ha! Bet you thought I'd gone for good.' The pain I felt then was almost physical. A deep, deep longing for Richard that nothing could touch.

After my mother died I had so many illnesses. Colds, flu. If any bug was going round, I'd pick it up. And I felt really tired too. It took so much energy just to do the things I had to do that I didn't have the strength for anything else.

My husband's death was so unnecessary, that's what's so hard to accept. It was sheer incompetence on the part of the hospital and the doctors he saw there. Eventually they admitted liability and settled out of court for a huge sum. But I don't want the money. I want my husband back. It happened four years ago, but I still feel angry. I'm angry at God too. He shouldn't have let it happen.

Grief takes as many different forms as there are people who are grieving. Everyone's experience is unique to them and there is no right or wrong way to get through it. But there are, of course, stages and reactions which are common to most people's experiences. For instance, grief can engender a strength of feeling that is unpredictable and can be frightening because of its sheer intensity. At other times it can create a disturbing absence of feeling—numbness and emptiness, a feeling of 'deadness'. Life becomes a routine of 'going through the motions'.

It is not particularly helpful to stipulate the stages of grieving along with some kind of time-scale. Most people do go through a period of denial at the beginning. But while it may only last a matter of hours for some, it may last months, or even years for others. So much depends on the circumstances of the death. Were we there? Was it expected? What was our relationship with the person? Also, so much depends on our age, our beliefs, our personality and our life experience. All these affect the way we grieve.

The other problem with talking about stages of bereavement is that it implies there is a straightforward process where anger follows denial and depression follows anger. There isn't such a clear-cut process. People swing from phase to phase, even years later.

What is important is to grasp that there is no right or wrong way to grieve. There is no order in which we ought to be feeling certain emotions, no time-scale we ought to follow. How we grieve is our own personal journey which we have to make alone. Of course there will be people and events along the way who may help us, and there may be other grieving people who are sharing the same loss. But how we work out and live through our own grief is unique to each of us.

In our normal lives, we generally draw strength from knowing that we are neither mad, nor odd or abnormal in the way we feel or think. We need to remember this when we grieve, particularly if we feel we ought to be getting over it. Professionals who spend a lot of time with the bereaved say that it takes roughly two years for someone to work through a major bereavement. This isn't to say that for two years we feel miserable and then we wake up one morning to find ourselves well again. What it is saying is that bereavement is a lengthy process. As time passes, the good spells will gradually get longer, the feelings will become less intense, the adaptation will get easier. But it is a process which takes time, and we proceed at our own pace.

Molly's story

Molly was sixty-two years old when her husband Mark died, three days after a severe heart attack.

I '*m glad we had those three days. Mark was weak, but not in a lot of pain, and so we were able to talk together. The children and grandchildren were able to see him and he was surrounded by so much love in those few days. I just had the feeling that he would never leave hospital, from the moment our doctor sent him in there. And I was right. Mark had been making good progress, and then he'd had another heart attack. They tried to resuscitate him but it was no good.*

Our son took care of all the arrangements and in the months ahead I was really grateful for his practical, down-to-earth help. He lives two hours away and he's got his own life and family, but he made it clear I could always phone up if I needed to know something. I was so glad he'd said that, because I was clueless. I'd never changed a light-bulb before, or a plug; and I used to get in such a panic about how to pay bills. I didn't know anything about bank giros, direct debits, standing orders. Mark had looked after all of that.

But I've got ahead of myself. How did I feel in the first few days and weeks after Mark died? It's so difficult to say! I felt so many things: disbelief, anger, resentment, fear, sadness. To begin with, I fell apart. I cried and cried, and how I ever got through the funeral I'll never know. I've always believed in God and got a lot of comfort from praying, but at the beginning, just after Mark had died, I couldn't pray at all. I was wrapped in a cocoon of grief and nothing could get through. I didn't have any words for what I felt, and when my family and friends talked to me, although I answered, I couldn't really hear what they'd said.

I wasn't hungry. I wasn't thirsty. If somebody gave me anything to eat or drink I'd take it, but I couldn't taste it. And I found that I could fall asleep quite easily but the dreams I had! Mark would be alive and well and we'd be planning things together, like a holiday or a house move. And then the plans would go wrong. I'd leave the passports behind, or the tickets; or I'd open the door of the new house and realize I didn't like it and wanted the old one back! These dreams were so vivid, and I'd feel so anxious and wake up really suddenly. To begin with I'd reach across the bed to find Mark to cuddle up to, and then be hit by the awful realization that he was dead. In the middle of the night, in the bed we'd shared for years, I would feel so alone, so desolate.

Night-time is still the worst, three years on. There's nothing more lonely than waking up in the middle of the night. It's the only time I feel scared in the house and I really have to steel myself to get up and walk downstairs if there's something I want. But these are the times I now use for prayer. Not always. Sometimes I just want company and so I switch on the radio. Thank God for those people who work through the night. They've a real ministry, but I don't suppose they see it like that.

During the day, it was about a month before I started to be able to do bits and pieces around the house. Even then, I'd walk into a room to do something and then forget why I'd gone in there. And the things I'd find in the fridge! One day I found a hairbrush which I'd put there by mistake. But there'd be all sorts of things happen in a day which would suddenly propel me into tears: mail which arrived for Mark, photographs I'd see when dusting, passing Mark's favourite chair.

My son and two daughters were so good. They were grieving too and we had tearful sessions together when we'd talk about things we'd done as a family, what Mark had said to them. And I'd tell them about when we first met and how my mother didn't think that Mark was good enough for me. But, of course, my children had their own responsibilities and it wasn't long before they had to go back to pick up their own lives. They all lived some distance away and couldn't just pop in, so there soon came a time when I was all on my own.

That first day, when I waved off the last of my children and shut the door behind me, I thought I'd die! The silence in the house was deafening. I didn't know what to do. I walked from room to room, touching things . . . straightening a cushion, smoothing a sheet. I put the radio on. I switched it off a few minutes later. I tried to watch TV. I walked away, leaving the set on. I went into the garden, pulled up a *few weeds, and then came back in again. I felt so aimless, so useless, and the day stretched ahead interminably.*

I could have gone out, but I was too scared. I didn't want to see people doing ordinary things, looking as if they hadn't a care in the world. I found the noise of the traffic disturbing too. It felt aggressive and I kept thinking it would get out of control and swerve on to the pavement and knock me over.

So I stayed indoors. But by the middle of the afternoon I couldn't bear it any longer and phoned up a friend to ask if she could come over. She stayed for a while. It helped, but then she had to leave, and a whole long evening loomed ahead.

By nine I could bear it no longer and went to bed. But sleep wouldn't come. I tossed and turned. I cried. I shouted at Mark, demanding to know why he'd left me like this, and then got frightened in case I was losing my mind. You shouldn't talk to the dead, I kept telling myself. It's not healthy! So, in the end I went downstairs and grabbed Mark's favourite whisky, took it back to the bedroom, and drank two large glasses of the stuff. I hate whisky normally, but that night, as it burned my throat every time I swallowed, it felt comforting.

There were lots of other days like that one. I realize now it's inevitable. You cannot possibly live with someone for forty-two years and not feel like you've had a limb amputated when they've gone. And, as a widowed friend of mine aptly puts it, it's like the limb was amputated without the benefit of anaesthetic. Your whole lifestyle is affected too. I never eat at the table normally. I put the plate on my knee and watch television while I eat. I don't go out as much either. The friends who used to ask Mark and I round together don't ask me on my own.

The worst thing still is the loneliness, even now. I've always lived with other people and these last three years on my own have been awful. You can do so many things: you can go to church, you can do voluntary work, you can go to exercise classes, you can meet friends for coffee. But you can't do them every hour of the day. At some point you have to come back, shut the door behind you, and be on your own. That's when the loneliness can hit. Not always. I'm now at the stage when I can enjoy my own company for a short time, but the loneliness still gets to me sometimes.

I don't find it easy to say this. Women of my age are from a generation where you don't talk about sex, but I so miss being touched by someone who loves me. Mark and I were hardly the world's greatest lovers, but when we made love I felt so safe and so wanted. Now I'm on my own and sometimes I just long to be held. I see couples walking along the street hand in hand, or kissing one another, and I get a stab of jealousy through me that feels like real pain. Or I look in the mirror and I see the lines on my face, the ones which Mark used to tell me were lines of experience and character forming, and I just feel old and unfeminine.

But I could be on my own for the next ten or twenty years. At the moment I feel useful because I can still get about and do things. I enjoy helping out as a volunteer at the local hospital, or going to stay with the children and keeping the grandchildren occupied. But there's going to come a day when age catches up and I won't have the same strength. I dread that happening, but it makes me think I've got to try and find ways of enjoying my own company more. It's not easy though.

Bereavement is always an isolating experience to some degree, but the death of a partner almost always leads to the worst kind of loneliness. Sometimes it is overwhelming. After many years of marriage, of sharing so much of our lives with someone else, it is very difficult indeed to get used to our own company. If we're younger and there are still children at home, then there will be other people around who need us. But if we are left to live on our own there can be a real sense of uselessness. With the death of a partner it is likely that we not only mourn someone we loved dearly, but that we also grieve the loss of our previous way of life.

All this assumes a loving relationship. Not all partnerships are that positive. Sometimes death will usher in feelings of release and freedom. After thirty or so years of an unsatisfactory, or even violent marriage, death is welcomed. In these circumstances perhaps the most difficult thing to handle is the guilt at feeling free.

Stages of bereavement

Although people are individuals and mourn in different ways and at different times, there are recognized stages of grief. Not everyone will go through them all, but the following are the most common. They do not necessarily come in this order, and they often overlap.

SHOCK

The word shock is self-explanatory, and in bereavement its cause is obvious. What is not so obvious is how it manifests itself. It may be expressed as denial—not believing what has happened; or numbness—a lack of feeling, impassively 'going through the motions' during the events that follow a death. Sometimes it feels as if the carpet has been pulled from under our feet.

Shock also brings with it feelings that we more normally associate with fear—'butterflies' in the stomach, loss of appetite, edginess. This is because when we feel threatened or alarmed about anything, our bodies release certain chemicals which are meant to help us to escape or fight an aggressor. This means that, over the longer period of acute stress which bereavement brings, our bodies are subject to surges of adrenalin. This can make us feel panicky and breathless.

Other physical symptoms related to shock include insomnia, loss of appetite, loss of weight, headaches, heartburn, a susceptibility to infection, clumsiness and lack of concentration.

It is also quite common to feel the same symptoms as the person who has died.

SEARCHING

If we have lost something we go searching for it. If a dog's owner goes away on holiday then the dog pines for its master. Pining in an animal is something we can recognize. It represents a strength of feeling which is more than just missing the owner.

The searching stage of bereavement comes when we ourselves look for the person who has died, pining because they cannot be found. We pine out of loyalty and emotion, just as the dog does for the master who has gone away. Rationally we know that there is no point in searching because we know the person is dead, but emotionally there is still a desire to keep on looking.

It's this searching instinct which leads to seeing the face of 'the lost one' in crowds or supermarkets or trains—some people touch and feel the clothes of the person who has died because the smell or the memory brings them closer to the one they've lost. Quite often people will talk of 'seeing' the dead person in the house, or 'hearing' them or even 'smelling' them. Such 'glimpses' can be frightening, but they are a normal reaction to loss. Sometimes the searching is evident in repeated visits to the cemetery, in the hope of finding the person again.

The restlessness felt by many bereaved people springs from this need to search. We are hardly likely to say that we need to look for the person who has died, we probably don't even see it as such, but deep within us we feel we ought to be doing something, but don't know what. It can be a preoccupying, all-consuming drive (if not a fully conscious one); so no wonder there is little inclination left for food, or work, or sleep, or even other family members.

ANGER

Anger and resentment are common. The anger comes because we need someone to blame for the loss we have sustained. It may be the doctors who become the targets. It may be ourselves, for something we did or did not do. It could be the estate agent, the solicitor, the bank manager. It might even be the deceased for 'walking out on us', or God for having 'taken away' the person we loved.

So much of our adult life is about being in control, or struggling to be in control, of our own lives. All being well, the maturer we become, the more possible it is to build a secure environment for ourselves and those we love. And then along comes death and snatches someone we love. Not only do we want them back and cannot have them, but we also lose a vital part of our security. And the result is that the world around us now feels unsafe, and we feel a great sense of loss. We are outraged, angry.

The anger we feel is often taken out on others around us. Irritability, a tendency to flare up over small things or pick quarrels, are manifestations of the underlying anger. Sometimes it's a passive anger which never gets expressed but comes out by our being unkind or malicious.

DEPRESSION

Depression is the normal human reaction to loss of any sort. Bereavement is such a large loss that it is not surprising that feelings of depression or sadness can last for a long time. The previous stages of shock, searching and anger are all initial reactions to a death. They occur because parts of us cannot yet believe or accept what has happened. Depression, however, comes when we accept the reality of the loss, and react to it.

Depression may take the form of crying bouts, tiredness, disturbance of normal sleep rhythms, loss of interest in things around us, or loss of concentration. One person described it as the world losing colour.

Despite the well-intentioned phrase 'snap out of it', depression is not something that people can just shake off. It is a physical and mental condition which takes time to heal. Sometimes it needs professional help from doctors, counsellors, or psychiatrists.

RESOLUTION

This is the stage when we somehow come to terms with, accept and adapt to the loss we have sustained. There may still be pangs of grief prompted by a photograph or a particular memory, but we have good memories too and can enjoy them. In no sense have we now forgotten the person who died, but we have lived and grown through the pain.

Knowing about these stages may be helpful when it comes to understanding the process of grief. But it is so important to remember that the whole thing is a process which people go through in different ways and at different times. We cannot tick off our searching phase and say, 'Right that's searching over, now let's tackle anger.'

Bereavement is not tidy as tidy as that because the reactions of human beings are complex. But one thing is certain: if we were newly bereaved and went to sleep for two years, we wouldn't wake up and find ourself magically in the resolution stage having missed all the pain and messiness that the other stages entail! We would still have to face up to the loss and find ways of living with it. It's not time in itself that is the great healer, but the passing of time during which we have the opportunity to grieve and come through the ordeal.

James' story

James' story is a sad and realistic account of his journey through grief as he came to terms with his wife Christine's death. At the time of her death they were both in their early forties and had no children.

Christine had been out for a run early one evening. She came back home, had a shower and then collapsed. She died in hospital later that night from a burst artery in the brain. James asked that her organs be donated for use in transplant surgery.

O n the outside I must have looked really in control. (They probably thought I was unfeeling.) But I'm used to taking charge and it just seemed to happen automatically. It was something to do, for heavens sake! I phoned our vicar and he gave me the number of Christine's parents' vicar, who I then phoned and asked to go round and tell them in person. They are elderly and I didn't want them just to hear by phone.

And that set the pattern for the next few days. I made myself really busy. Inside I kept getting these surges of feeling which were horrendous, as if I was really afraid about something or nervous about giving the biggest and most important speech of my career. I couldn't sleep very much either. I kept going over what had happened. Time after time, my brain kept giving me the action replay and it was impossible to hit the stop button.

Christine and I had been married for eight years and before that I'd lived on my own for over ten years, so being on my own in the house didn't worry me. In fact I didn't want people coming round because they reminded me of why they were there, and what had happened. At least when I was on my own I could 'pretend' Christine wasn't dead and was just away for a few days.

It was strange the way I kept expecting her to walk through the door. Or I'd walk into the bathroom in the morning and be surprised that there wasn't a damp towel lying on the floor. (Christine always got to the shower before me and I used to get really annoyed that she'd just leave the towel lying on the floor.) Who'd have thought that I'd actually miss tripping over it!

I found myself playing Christine's favourite CDs in the evening or just sitting holding the silk dress which she'd had made when we visited Hong Kong for a short holiday. And one night I even sprayed the pillow with that incredibly expensive perfume that she insisted on using every day. The smell of it, even now, reminds me of Christine.

For months I kept all of her things exactly where she'd left them. Her clothes hung in the wardrobe, her make-up stayed in the bathroom. I couldn't bear to get rid of them. In fact I needed them there because to remove them would be like removing the last trace of Christine and I wasn't ready for that.

Was I angry? Oh yes! There were times when I blamed Christine for 'running away'—opting out of the human race. I know she didn't, there's no way she chose to die, but sometimes that's what I thought. Maybe if she hadn't been such a keen jogger she'd still be alive! All that running can't have been good for somebody who already had a weakness in a blood-vessel. But then she didn't know she had a time bomb sitting in her brain so I can't really blame her!

Sometimes I'd feel guilty that we were both so caught up in our careers that we didn't spend enough time together. If I'd known we'd only be married for such a short time then I'm sure things would have been different. We might even have decided to try and have children. It's funny, isn't it, how you hear of fatal accidents and illnesses happening to other people but you never really think it might happen to you? I'm sure I thought we'd both live out our three score years and ten!

Within a fortnight of Christine's death I was back at work. I was desperate to get back though I didn't know why. Now when I look back I can see that work at least was somewhere familiar. The people hadn't changed, the job hadn't changed. In short, it was security. With Christine gone my whole life had been turned upside down and work was the part of my life which was still the same. Perhaps I was running away too, running away from the terrible changes I faced at home.

I had terrible difficulty seeing anything through. I'd start tasks and not finish them. When I was dictating letters I kept losing my place. I couldn't concentrate at all. Yet I'd be the first one into the office in the morning and the last to leave at night. Deep down I suppose I didn't want to go home to face the emptiness there. And I was incredibly ratty too! So many little things just seemed to set my nerves on edge. Laughter in the office, or things not going completely to plan, or even the phone ringing.

The guys in the office would invite me to join them for drinks after work but I didn't want to. And at weekends I'd mope around the house, not wanting to do anything or go anywhere. I would sit mindlessly in front of the TV set, flicking from channel to channel. It was months before I was able to enjoy that time to myself, and it was then that I found I was able to go back to church occasionally. But I felt like a fish out of water there. There were no other men of my age there on their own and I felt terribly conspicuous.

Then, just after Christmas (I can't talk about Christmas—it was dreadful; I've never felt so alone in my life), the vicar asked if I'd host one of the Lent study groups. I was about to say no, like I did to everything else, when I found myself saying yes. The first Thursday the group was to meet I made sure there was some decent coffee in the house, and plenty of biscuits. With a shock I realized it was the first time since Christine had died that I'd invited people to the house.

There were seven of us there that night, following a course that was looking at prayer. I'm certainly no expert, but then no one else was either (including the vicar, or so he said!). But the discussion we had was honest and thought-provoking, and I found I actually enjoyed it. Also, we were a very diverse group. There was a lovely couple in their seventies who I only knew by sight, a teenager and her friend from another church completely, and a professional couple who were new to the area. After everyone had gone I realized that no one there had known Christine and I'd been able to relate to them as me.

That was an important discovery because as the course continued, and afterwards, I realized that I was having to build a life which was mine, and not mine and Christine's. I could never replace Christine but I had to adapt to her not being around any more. At work that had been easy because she had never been a part of that world, but outside work it took me a good year or so to find things to fill the gap Christine had left behind.

James' story reveals some of the key moments and issues in his journey through grief and by the end shows how he is moving towards some kind of acceptance. But it is possible to get stuck on the way and to hit a point which you cannot get beyond. This was what Anna experienced.

Anna's story

Anna was sixteen when her mother died after a short illness, aged forty. The family were all members of a large, evangelical, charismatic church and the funeral for Anna's mother produced a packed church.

There was lots of triumphalist singing but the one thing I remember above everything else is the pastor's address. He looked down at me, held my eye and said, 'Sister, don't mourn for your mother. She's gone to a much better place. God has called her home. Praise the Lord!' And I sat there, desperately wanting my mother, yet trying not to cry because the pastor had told me I shouldn't be mourning.

Every time I felt the tears beginning, for months afterwards, I just remembered the pastor's words and prayed that God would forgive me for still missing my mother. Obviously I was a selfish Christian, as I could not be happy that my mother was in heaven! And the time passed, slowly, as I tried to tame what I was feeling and not let it show. Over the years I got pretty good at it too, except I kept the lid on so tightly I don't think I let myself feel anything.

Then, when I was about twenty, I was back at my dad's for a weekend. On Saturday afternoon a neighbour walked into our garden carrying Rosie, the cat which had been mine since she was a kitten. Rosie was dead, knocked down by a car, and our neighbour had found her lying in the road. I went berserk. Crying, sobbing and it just wouldn't stop. A doctor was called. I was given some pills to swallow and drifted off to sleep. But when I came to, I remembered Rosie, thought of Mum and decided that life was all about death, so I might just as well get it over with. Seemingly I raided the medicine cabinet and swallowed whatever I could find—not that I remember much of that. The next thing for me was waking up in hospital the next day.

It was recommended that I see a psychiatrist, but as there were volunteers wandering around the ward inviting people to the chapel for a service, I found myself asking to speak to the chaplain. I still don't know why I was so insistent, but he came along a few hours later, and he helped me so much. I told him all that had happened and he very gently asked me if my picture of God had room for any love in it. I was about to say that of course it did when I had the image of an

48

authoritarian headmaster pop into my head, holding my mother against her will. It shook me, but instead of suppressing it as usual, I talked about it.

That was the beginning of a long journey back to life. I saw the psychiatrist and on his advice, and the chaplain's, booked myself in for therapy with a Christian therapist who specialized in bereavement. My father was appalled, telling me that God had all the answers I'd ever need, but I persevered.

And I'm so glad I did. I was able to see that faith or no faith, I had every right to grieve for my mother. I'd loved my mother and no matter where she had gone, it was normal to feel loss and separation and grief. God didn't create us as he did, and Jesus didn't urge us to love one another with a quality love, only to deny our feelings of grief when death separates us. Grief is the price we pay for loving.

I also saw how, for the four years between Mum's death and my breakdown, I had done little other than 'exist'. I'd used up so much energy just trying to deny my grief that there wasn't any left for anything else. And by denying my grief, it hadn't gone away, I'd just buried it deep within. So when Rosie had been run over, all that bottled-up, unexpressed grief just exploded out.

Since then, working with my therapist, I've faced the grief I felt over Mum's death. It wasn't easy and the pain was still there, but I had to express it in order to move on. And I have moved on. I enjoy life so much more. I've got more energy and I can look at my garden and see all the signs of new life around and truly praise God for all he has taught me, through the therapist and others. My faith is stronger and deeper, but it recognizes that as human beings we also have lives to live. Lives that are based on the here and now and not the future.

Although Anna's experience of being told that she shouldn't mourn came from a particular Christian understanding, there are people who, for other reasons, find they have never completed their grieving, sometimes years afterwards. As in Anna's case, it may be the death of a pet, or some other loss (redundancy, illness, break-up of marriage) that becomes the trigger to release the pent-up grief. The reaction to the second loss might appear excessive and out of all proportion to the scale of the loss, and this is because it has begun to release the feelings that were blocked after the first loss.

In other situations, the period of mourning may be going on indefinitely, with no resolution following the bereavement. This can happen if the mourner had lived vicariously through the person who has since died. Take the example of a parent who was living the life he would have liked through his child. If that child dies tragically when young, there may be difficulty in moving through to acceptance, because the parent has lost his own 'future' too. Or imagine a widow whose entire adult life had been bound up with her husband's. If she had no independent life of her own before his death, she may be unable to build a new life after it because she is still grieving. Not only has she lost her husband, she has also lost her identity as 'the husband's wife'.

If you feel that you would like to talk to someone about the grief or anger or depression that you still feel as the result of a death, no matter how long ago, then there are people you can approach. Ask your GP, or the Citizen's Advice Bureau for details of local bereavement services. Or you could find out if there is a hospice nearby. Staff who work in hospices care not just for their dying patients but their relatives, before and after the death. They will be sympathetic to your wish to talk and even if it is not possible for you to attend there, staff will be able to direct you to other organizations or a bereavement counsellor.

Alternatively, there is a list of organizations at the back of this book. Every single one of them is there to be contacted—for information, advice, or the chance to talk. The majority of them are not there to offer professional counselling, but to 'befriend' and listen. They can also offer the opportunity to meet other people who have suffered a similar loss. Don't be shy about getting in touch, because sometimes just talking to other people who feel a bit like you do can make all the difference. You might also read the later chapter, 'Putting the pieces back together again', because it describes how others have done just that.

4

A GIFT OF TIME
Facing terminal illness

When my wife's illness was diagnosed as terminal cancer, she wanted to discuss the situation with me and the children. This she did, and afterwards we did not dwell on the inevitable but took each day as it came. It was just five weeks until she died and during that time we discussed how I would manage without her, and I promised I would go to see the places we had planned to visit together.

My only regret looking back is that we never talked about what was happening to him. I feel that if we had talked then, maybe things would be easier now. I feel that you must be told if somebody near to you has a terminal illness because I feel that I was never really told this until two days before his death.

Through the hospice I have been encouraged to talk with the children about their father dying; and even though they do not want their father to die, they accept that he would be best to die, rather than go through any more pain and suffering.

Although none of us knows when we are going to die, when someone is found to have a terminal illness, there is a sense in which it can be seen as a gift of time. A strange thought? Well, yes—initially. But when the shock of the bad news lessens, the idea of a gift of time emerges. Instead of 'if only', as is so often repeated in circumstances of sudden death (if only I'd told him I loved him ... if only I'd said I was sorry), a diagnosis of terminal illness offers a gift of real quality time. There will be opportunities to talk, to share memories, to say things that need and want to be said. Knowing that death is only days, weeks or months away can radically reduce the 'if only' issues left.

And that is why there is a place for a chapter on terminal illness in a book that is about bereavement, because the process of 'successful' bereavement is about finally letting go—letting go of all the things that tie you to the person who has died. It's not that you forget that you ever loved them, but that you are able to treasure that love in a positive way. It sometimes takes years, but in the terrible situation of being told that a loved one has a terminal illness which is now beyond any further medical intervention, there is this curious paradox of 'a gift of time' which can help people to let go.

Mary's story

Mary was fifty-five years old and working full-time as a teacher when her husband, Sam, collapsed at home with severe chest pains. She immediately feared that he was having a heart attack and called out the family doctor. The doctor disagreed. What Sam had, he thought, was severe muscle strain and it required rest. But Mary had been worried about Sam for weeks. He'd lost weight and seemed very tired. She pointed all this out to the doctor and it was arranged that Sam would go to see a specialist at the local hospital.

X-rays revealed a shadow on one of the lungs and so, a fortnight later, Sam underwent a bronchoscopy, an examination which allows doctors to pass a tube into the lungs and see directly what the cause of the shadow may be. The news was grim. Sam had advanced lung cancer and there was nothing further that could be done medically.

Mary maintains that she will never forget the day she found

out. It was a beautiful spring day, a clear blue sky, fresh green leaves on the trees—the kind of day on which you feel glad to be alive. She and Sam were enjoying the warm sun out in the garden when their family doctor called round to tell them the news.

I was numb. I just could not take it in. Sam was ultra-calm, asking the doctor matter-of-factedly about how long he had left; and didn't react when the doctor replied that nobody really knew. It could be as little as three months, as much as two years. Quite simply, the doctor said, the best thing is to take each day as it comes and to make the most of it.

After the doctor left, we went indoors and sat on the sofa. We'd left the patio doors open and the sounds of the world that had seemed so normal just a short time before, washed over us as we sat there just holding one another tightly. We cried, we kissed, and Sam, who's not normally a romantic man, told me how much he loved me. I remember hearing the wind rustling in the trees outside and praying silently to God that he would give me the strength to get through all this, and that he'd make things easy and pain-free for Sam.

Sam and Mary were both actively involved in their local church and so asked their vicar to visit them as soon as he could. He came that night, deeply upset himself, as Sam and he had become friends despite their heated differences about modern church music. Together they chatted, cried and even laughed a little, and then the three of them prayed together—not for long, because the emotions were so raw and so confusing that it was hard to know quite what to pray for. But they sat, heads bowed with Mary and Sam holding hands, as their vicar asked for God's presence to be with them and that they would be sure of his love for them throughout the days and weeks ahead.

Mary said it was difficult for her to sleep that night, although Sam did. As she lay there beside him hearing the distant clock chiming the hours of the long dark night, she cried silent tears, confused about why God had let this happen to them. Occasionally she reached out to stroke Sam's hair, unable to comprehend that at some short time in the future he wasn't going to be there any more.

I must have slept eventually because I remember waking up feeling OK. Then, a split second later, I had this awful wave of sickening reality hit me. I should have gone to school that day but I called in sick. But two days later I was back to work and so was Sam.

Sometimes I found myself thinking that maybe the doctors had got the results muddled up, but it was only two weeks before Sam was unable to work, and before my very eyes I could see him getter thinner and weaker. We cried many tears during the next few weeks: tears for ourselves and for a lot of 'might-have-beens'. I realized that Sam would never see any grandchildren we might have, and we'd been talking a lot about going on a grand tour round the world when he retired in a few years' time. That was obviously not going to happen now. I also thought of the plants and vegetables we'd been planting the day that the doctor called and found myself crying because Sam would probably never see them full-grown. The laugh of it all, is that he didn't really like gardening anyway.

But we had some good times too. We'd told the children the news straight away and although they were both living away from home they came back to visit as often as they could. Friends from church and work came round a lot as well. Sometimes I wanted Sam to myself and resented the fact that he would put on a a brave face for them and then all I would get would be an exhausted, sleepy husband. But he enjoyed their visits and I suppose I still got a lot of time with him really.

Within six weeks, though, he became very weak and I took leave from work to be able to nurse him at home. A district nurse came in every morning, our family doctor was very good at visiting, and towards the end a Macmillan nurse came every evening as well.

Each day was precious to us, but we needed some kind of normality too. The television helped, a window on a sometimes needed outside world. But sometimes we just sat and talked sharing memories about when we first met and some of the antics of the children when they were younger.

But Sam wanted to talk about the future as well and made me promise I wouldn't hang on to the house after he died if I didn't want to. He checked too that I knew about all the bills that were to be paid and about bank accounts and insurance policies and where his will was.

We also talked about his funeral. He chose the hymns he wanted to be sung, determined that we would all sing 'Thine be the Glory', and asked that after he was cremated his ashes be scattered on lake Windermere, because that was where he had first felt that there really was a God.

During all this time together we became very close, but we also found a great deal of comfort in prayer. Our vicar would come to give us communion once a week, and that was a very special time for all of us. I felt as if in some way it was helping hand Sam over into God's safe keeping and we both always felt very peaceful afterwards.

It was also a time of voyage. My grieving began the moment I knew that Sam had terminal cancer and so, during the weeks we had together, I was learning to say goodbye, beginning to let go of him. And he was doing the same, preparing to face whatever lay ahead, because no matter how strong our faith, nobody really knows what happens after death, do they? He had to go on to the next stage alone and he also needed to learn to let go. As we learned to part from one another I find it hard to describe, but there were moments when it was really beautiful. We were completely honest with each other and there was no pretence.

Sam stayed at home throughout his illness, thanks to wonderful local nursing support, but in the last few hours he slipped into a coma and I just sat beside him holding his hand. His breathing got very loud and there were long gaps between each breath, but he was very peaceful. I thought I would be frightened, but I wasn't. And then Sam took one last deep breath, and then, almost like a whisper, the breath was released, and all the muscles of his face relaxed, and I realized Sam had gone. Very quietly. Very gently.

The children were there at the very end as they had both said they wanted to be. They'd been back with us for a couple of days, and when the nursing staff told us they thought Sam's death would be very soon we took it in turns to sit with him. But at the moment when he died we were all there, and I was so glad that we were all together. It was such an intimate moment and one that I don't think any of us will ever forget. It was also a very peaceful death and I think it helped us all to see that death needn't be frightening.

By the time Sam died, I think I was ready for his death. I was appalled by how ravaged his body had become, his need for powerful pain relief, and the indignity forced upon him by no longer being able *to look after himself. My strong, supportive other half who I'd always relied on to be there, was now completely dependent, and that's very hard to deal with. And although I've talked about how close we became during his illness I don't want to disguise how ghastly it can be as well. At times I felt revulsion at what the cancer had done to his body, but Sam felt that too. We didn't talk about it much, but we were honest about it when we did, and then quickly moved on to talk about other things.*

Although it was dreadful to see Sam's body literally wasting before my eyes I'm selfishly grateful that he died this way. Whenever I read of people who've lost loved ones through sudden death I can sense the enormous shock and disbelief they must feel. But I know that Sam was ready for death when it came. It was a release, and the weeks that led to it gave us a chance to share so much, and to learn to part. Also I'm grateful that Sam was able to help me practically. I'd always left financial matters to him, but he made sure I knew about how to sort out the life insurance, and helped me see what I'd need to do after his death. At the time I'd rather not have discussed it—it seemed tasteless, but he was right to force me to think about it all, because as he rightly guessed I wouldn't have had a clue!

Mary's experience of her husband's death could be called a good one—if there can ever be such a thing as a good experience where death is concerned. She can look back to that time they had together and experience very few regrets. The closeness and intimacy of those last few weeks are a very precious memory for her and she was very grateful that she was able to care for Sam at home right up to his death.

Obviously I grieved for Sam after his death. There were some long and lonely, painful times. Even now, three years later, I still miss him. I catch myself wondering what Sam would have thought of something that's happened. Like when the Berlin Wall came down. Sam would have loved that.

But I know that having that time together really helped me get through this whole thing they call bereavement. The important thing about it was that we were able to talk in a way that we really hadn't done before. Our love was very strong when he died, and if the whole ghastly experience of seeing a loved one die means anything at all, it means experiencing a very special and pure quality of human loving. It wasn't just between Sam and I, but with the children, and with all our friends who were there right the way through—cooking meals, bringing books, finding all sorts of ways to let us know that we were not forgotten. I think that's how I know God was with us through it all. He was there in that very special quality of loving that the children and I experienced; and selfish though it is, I do thank God that we had what truly was a gift of time.

This century, one material development in the area of terminal illness has been the hospice movement. Hospices are the result of the downside of scientific breakthroughs in the treatment of disease (and the consequent longer life expectancy in the so-called First World countries), and have come to mean that death does not need to represent defeat, and that dying people do not need to be forgotten.

One of the pioneers of the hospice movement was Elizabeth Kubler-Ross, a remarkable woman who believed passionately that society should recognize death as part of life. It was she who first used the phrase 'dealing with the unfinished business'.

This phrase sounds like the kind of sociological jargon that makes us cringe, yet it represents a crucial part of the opportunity offered by a terminal illness. The time that is left can become an opportunity to get things sorted out—emotionally as well as practically.

Emotionally, it may mean talking about embarrassing or shaming things that have never before been discussed. Incidents which happened years ago may have bred resentment and bad will ever since. It may be a time to ask or seek forgiveness for broken relationships, spiteful jealousies, even for abuse—sexual, mental or physical. And it is also a time to let people know what probably goes unsaid much of the time, that they are loved just as they are.

Practically, 'dealing with the unfinished business' may mean sorting out what should become of the home, or making sure that a will has been made which reflects the wishes of the person who is soon to die, or even planning the funeral service.

There is also time to anticipate some of the smaller details. The reality of life in late twentieth century Britain is that dealing with the death of someone close brings with it bureaucracy and procedures and paper work—all at a time when we are least able to think rationally about it. The kinds of contacts that need to be made after a death are not just with relatives and friends, doctors, undertakers and ministers; there are also banks, building societies, insurance companies, solicitors, electricity and gas and telephone companies, and the list goes on.

These details may sound trivial, and in some ways they are, but with the time warning offered by terminal illness at least there is an opportunity to find out where important documents are stored. Calculating though it seems, it does mean that the administrative tasks surrounding a death can happen more smoothly. The days ahead are going to be traumatic enough without the added burden of legal disputes and wranglings.

Lastly, while the 'unfinished business' is about practical and emotional matters, it is also about spiritual considerations as well.

A few years ago, people used to debate whether those with a terminal illness should be told about it. Now there is a greater acceptance that it is better for the patient and the relatives to know. Those who work with the dying say that patients intuitively sense they will die soon, even if nothing has been said to them. At least when everyone knows the severity of a loved one's condition, choices can be made about how to use the time that is left.

This time will be an emotional and spiritual roller-coaster, whether it is days, weeks or months. In the early days there will be a lot of disbelief: 'The doctors gave me the wrong results ... it's not as bad as they think.' In between there will be moments of immense anguish and bleakness, and cries of 'Why me, God? Why now?' (This, of course, is a generalization and if we could learn just one thing about bereavement and grief, then it is that everyone's experience is unique to them. There is no right or wrong way to grieve, no typical pattern to follow.)

But in terminal illness, the time is there for everyone involved. And for the Christian, or the person of another faith, or the person who simply feels that now is the moment finally to confront the spiritual nature of life, it can be 'extra time' to turn to God and, if necessary, make things right.

In some strands of the Christian Church confession and absolution are a normal part of the Christian life; in others the notion is alien. But beneath all strands there is an understanding that human beings are not perfect creatures and that the life, death and resurrection of Jesus opened up a new relationship with God that is there for the asking. So this gift of time, almost regardless of where the person stood before the illness occurred, is a chance to get things straight with God and maybe, as a result, with other people.

It may be important to ask forgiveness of God for a particular relationship which has been destructive and unloving: perhaps a child left home after a serious row and has remained distant ever since. It may be less dramatic: perhaps a relationship might just have been different. It is a cliché to say that the clock can never be put back. Of course it can't. But the time that is left can be used to improve matters for whatever period is left. Asking forgiveness from God is one thing, but it may also involve getting in touch with the person who has been the subject of so much heartache and bad feeling and asking their forgiveness too.

In a spiritual sense this gift of time may also be an opportunity to open up to God in a way that has never happened before. Even people who have gone to church Sunday in, Sunday out, year in, year out, may find their faith completely rocked by the news that a loved one is to die shortly. God can become a habit rather than a challenge, and it may take something earth-shattering like this to force us to think about what we believe deep down.

It may become a frightening time because suddenly our faith isn't as strong as we thought. Or we may get angry at God for letting this happen, or doubt whether God is even there, or think that God has in some way wished this on us because we haven't been good enough. These are all perfectly legitimate reactions; where loss is concerned, there are no right or wrong feelings or beliefs. We feel what we feel and we believe what we believe, and these feelings and beliefs can change from day to day, even hour to hour.

The important, steadying factor in all of this is God's rock-like and continuous love for us, no matter how desperate and weak we feel. It is love which is freely offered and freely given, and it comes because he also shares the pain and the anguish that are an inseparable part of loving.

And in all our anguish, we can become closer to God than we have ever been before. Imminent death focuses our minds on the essential elements of life. Suddenly things pale into insignificance that used to seem so important, such as where to go on holiday or the fact that the next-door neighbour keeps parking her car in front of our house. Instead, the things that are spotlighted are those parts of life which we know we are going to miss like crazy: friends, relatives, country walks on clear autumn days, laughter, love, and all those things which make it so good to be alive. Life, with all its ups and downs, seems a very precious gift indeed, and with that sense of preciousness comes a deep, deep appreciation of the Giver, the Creator of it all.

While we may value the spiritual present, we may also anticipate the spiritual future. What is life after death going to be like? Just as we had no notion before we were born of what life beyond the womb would be like, so we can barely imagine anything new after death. We simply have to trust that it is better and closer to the absolute Love that created us and called our world into being.

At this point, it probably won't mean a lot to use classical theological words such as heaven, salvation and eternal glory. If we want to, of course, each of us can read the Old and New Testaments and ask God to show us, even to reassure us, about what life means and what is in store for us beyond the grave. But a better aim would be to search for complete honesty, with each other and with God. It's a time to search with an urgency we may never have known before. And it's also a time to grow into the closer presence of God which normal life doesn't always permit.

Linda's story

Linda was in her mid-twenties when her mother was diagnosed

as having the horrific, paralyzing disease of the nervous system, motor neurone disease.

S he wasn't too bad to begin with and I didn't realize how awful the disease could be. Because she looked OK I tried to forget that she was ill and to get on with my own life. I've always been terrified of illness and hospitals, and I suppose I just didn't want to face up to the fact that Mum would die soon.

I realized I was finding excuses for why I couldn't go round for tea, and dreaded picking up the phone in case she was on the other end. Inside I felt guilty that I was doing this, but I also felt angry with her that she'd gone and got this dreadful disease. Then, one day, my boyfriend challenged me on what I was doing. He called me some things which really hurt and we had a monumental row. He told me how his father had died in an accident at his work, and how to this day he felt awful that they'd had words the last time he'd seen his dad alive.

I hated Jimmy then for what he said to me, but once my temper cooled I realized the truth of what he'd said. Next evening I went round to Mum's and for the first time could see how she must be feeling—facing a dreadful illness, divorced, and her only child now finding all sorts of reasons not to visit.

We began to talk, and she told me all sorts of things about her childhood and early days of marriage that I never knew. Then she talked about her death and of how frightened she felt. I didn't know what on earth to say and in the end all I could do fling my arms round her and we cried together.

Over the next two years Mum became more and more disabled. For some time I moved back in with her, but she soon needed more nursing care than I could give. It was then that she began to talk about suicide and euthanasia. At first the thought horrified me, but the more I saw her fear of what might lay ahead—losing her speech, unable to swallow, I began to think she had a point. I made her promise, though, that she wouldn't do anything without telling me. Even so, whenever I came in at night I dreaded finding that she'd gone ahead and ended her own life.

By now I also faced a decision about how best to care for Mum. I was already taking time off from work, and although they were sympathetic, I couldn't see the sympathy lasting for long. The choice seemed to be giving up work altogether, or getting Mum into a decent nursing home. We talked about it and she said that she didn't want me to ruin my career for her, and besides she'd feel more comfortable in a home.

The first time I had to leave her in that home I felt such enormous guilt. What sort of daughter was I to put her career before her mother? The staff there all assured me I was doing the right thing, but that night when I went off to bed and realized that I wouldn't have to waken in the night to help Mum to the loo, I felt such relief. And with the relief, back came the guilt.

Mum hated that home. For a week she kept putting on a brave face, and then one day I dropped by at lunch-time and found her in a dreadful state. It was then that she told me she wanted to come home or, failing that, to die. It felt like blackmail and whilst I can't say I hated her for doing it to me, I wasn't far off hate. I just didn't know what to do. I knew I couldn't cope with her at home, but I couldn't bear to see her so desperate. It wasn't that I didn't love her, she just needed so much care now and I knew that she'd never be able to get it if she came home.

Mum died a month later, after contracting pneumonia. I don't think she ever forgave me for not taking her home, and when I visited during those last weeks, the easy relationship we'd had before became strained. When she looked at me, with piercing dark eyes, I felt she was judging me and found me wanting. So many people have told me I did the right thing, but it spoiled those last days together.

We'd shared so much before then, but at the end it was like one of those awkward goodbyes at railway stations, willing the train to leave so that you don't have to struggle to make any more small talk to cover the discomfort. And then as soon as the train leaves you remember things that you meant to say.

Linda knows there were no other options for her, but still has enormous sadness that she and her mother weren't reconciled.

Deep down I'm grateful that when Mum first became ill I came to know her as a person, and not a mum, if you know what I mean. And I recognize that towards the end neither of us could quite face *up to the parting. For Mum, going home meant putting the clock back and getting better; and for me that time in the nursing home was when I could distance myself from the awfulness of her illness. It's just I wish that she could have died content, and I know she wasn't. One part of her was ready to die because she hated being so disabled, but the other still wanted to live. And even if I had that time over again, I don't know how I could have made it any different.*

Linda's experience of a gift of time was mixed. She was able to draw closer to her mother, but she regretted that her mother's last few weeks appeared to be so unhappy. And there is a danger when people speak almost romantically of a gift of time. It can set up false expectations—practical, emotional and spiritual.

Nevertheless, this is time that we can spend as we wish, and as we feel, with the person who is dying. The last days together may be a remarkable time of emotional and spiritual sharing, though they may be marred by pain or partially unresolved anger and resentment. Or it may be that we long so much for the suffering to end that we pray for death to come soon. To do so is not to reject the gift of time, for it is a loving response to want to see an end to suffering.

The question is whether the last days of the dying could have been better than they were. But we need to avoid wishful thinking. Deaths such as these are tough. And just because someone is dying, they don't necessarily become saintly and sweet, devoid of the weaknesses and strengths for which they have been loved. Arrangements for nursing care need to be appropriate and realistic, as does the amount of care we can give ourselves. What we can do depends on so many things, and we must be open to give and to listen without impossible goals. It would be sad to force the pace so that the dying person became resentful; it is better to be sensitive to their wishes, and to speak of our love for them.

The gift of time is different for everyone. A young New Zealand woman who was dying from leukaemia wrote a 'Letter to the Living' which she asked her brother to read aloud at her funeral. It was a remarkable letter and began with the words that follow;

they are included here as a fitting way to end this chapter.

*A**s the prospect of dying grows closer I am constantly wondering what it holds in store for me. I choose to believe that it will not be an ending but a transition from one state to another, from a physical reality to a spiritual one. Twenty years ago I purchased my ticket for this life; now the time has come to hand it back and move on to new challenges and new joys. Death holds no horror for me.*

5

'I NEVER EVEN SAID GOODBYE'
Sudden death

*It was almost midnight when the doorbell rang. Two
police officers were there. 'Mrs Green?' I nodded. 'Can we
come in?' They were ill at ease and I suddenly felt very
cold. 'It's bad news, I'm afraid. We have reason to believe
your husband was killed in a pile-up on the motorway
late this evening.' No, it couldn't be. I'd only spoken to
him on the phone at six. There had to be some mistake.
But there wasn't!*

---

*I came home from work and discovered my two-year-old
daughter in her playpen, crying. The television was on but
Jayne, my wife, was nowhere to be seen. I called and
called but no answer. I put my head into the kitchen and
there she was. Lying on the floor. It was a massive brain
haemorrhage, I was told later. Nothing anyone could have
done, they said. Inside, I scream and scream, silently!*

---

*Our son Jacob went into hospital for a routine operation.
Next thing I know he's in Intensive Care on a life-support
machine. Two long days and nights we sat there, willing
him to live, but there was no hope. We donated his organs
'cause he'd have wanted us to do that. He'd have been
eighteen next week.*

I've often heard people say, 'When my number's up, I want to go
suddenly. Here one minute, gone the next! Much the best way to

go.' The thought has certain attractions: no pain, no worry, no time to think what we might miss. For the people left behind, however, the shock is enormous. When we wave goodbye to a perfectly healthy person and only hours later hear of their death, it is very difficult to believe. Suddenly we are thrown into a world of post-mortems, inquests, coroners, registrars, undertakers. Not only is there no warning of the death, no time to adjust or begin to prepare, but a sudden or accidental death has to be shared not just with the others who mourn but with the legal world as well.

In the midst of what is probably the most shocking event we have ever encountered, the law demands that there are certain circumstances in which a medical certificate of the cause of death cannot be issued. In these instances, deaths must be reported to a coroner. For many of us the word 'coroner' belongs to the world of TV fiction because it is often the first point of contact in a detective story where foul play is suspected. So to hear that a certificate of cause of death cannot be issued until a coroner has been consulted is at best alarming, and at worst terrifying.

There is a wide range of circumstances in which a death must be notified to a coroner:

☐ If a doctor did not see the person who has died in the 14 days prior to death (28 days in Northern Ireland).

☐ If the death occurred during an operation or within 24 hours of one.

☐ If the death was sudden, accidental, inexplicable or suspicious.

☐ If the death might have been related to, or caused by, industrial disease.

☐ If the death was caused or accelerated by injuries received during military service.

The involvement of the coroner may just be a formality but it is the coroner's decision whether or not a post-mortem or an inquest is necessary. It is not the coroner's job to determine civil or criminal liabilities, but to establish the cause of death. Only when the coroner is satisfied about the cause of death can a death certificate be issued.

Just reading the list and noting the legal phraseology feels forbidding. No wonder relatives can feel completely out of their depth at a time when they are already in deep shock.

Joan's story

It was just this kind of living nightmare that Joan found herself in. She was twenty-nine and had just moved two hundred miles north to be with her husband who was starting a new job there. They had recently moved into a new home with a £60,000 mortgage and had ploughed virtually all of their savings into new furniture, curtains and carpets. It felt like the dream home they had always wanted. They had agreed that Joan would wait a few months before finding herself a job locally so that she could get to know the area and make the new house feel like home.

*T*wo months after we moved in, Chris came home from work with a splitting headache and a really sore back. One of his colleagues from work was due to come for dinner that night. Chris wanted me to get to meet new people, so he was loath to call off the dinner. Instead he took some painkillers and soon began to feel better.

The dinner went well although Chris didn't eat very much. He drank quite a lot of wine, joking that it was purely medicinal. By bedtime he looked a bit rough and was running a temperature, but said he'd just take some more painkillers and he'd be right as rain by tomorrow. In bed I cuddled up to him, kissed him and thanked him for helping me meet new people.

Those turned out to be the last words I spoke to him. Next morning I found him dead beside me. Even now, four years on, I can't describe what I felt or even what I did. I'm told I dialled 999 but I don't remember.

My parents and Chris' came to stay with me. It was awful, just awful. There was a post-mortem to see why he'd died and then I was asked questions about how much he'd drunk and how many pills he'd taken. Had he been upset and was he worried about anything? The penny clicked. They wanted to know if my husband had taken his own life. No he didn't, I screamed at them.

I couldn't understand why they wouldn't let us hold the funeral. I just wanted to get away from it all, but then, after all sorts of tests (I shudder every time I think of them cutting Chris' body into bits) they said he'd died from a rare but virulent virus. The alcohol and the painkillers had been contributory factors, or something like that.

The whole thing became even more of a nightmare. Chris hadn't left a will, he said there was plenty of time for that! There was a problem with the life insurance and they said they wouldn't pay up, so I'd either have to make the mortgage payments or the house would be repossessed. The car was taken back by his company. Chris' family blamed me for his death and one of his sisters started sending me hate mail. It was all too much for me. A doctor put me on to tranquillizers and sleeping pills, and if it hadn't been for my parents I think I would just have swallowed the whole lot and gone to join Chris.

Eventually, the insurance firm changed its mind, but the house was nearly sold anyway by then. I hated it. The brand new things which I'd really wanted in our new home just mocked me.

One year on, I was a wealthy zombie living with its parents. I had no friends, I didn't want to go out. I lived on pills to stop me feeling and other pills to make me sleep. My parents were at their wits' end. I couldn't cry, I couldn't concentrate on anything for more than a few minutes, and I could sit in the same chair for hours just gazing out the window.

Then one day Mum came into my bedroom and said she'd arranged for me to go and see a counsellor. I just nodded. I'd agree to anything just to be left in peace. But two days later I went to the counsellor and began what I now see was my first step back to life.

It took a long, long time. I'd become addicted to the tranquillizers, and kicking that was bad enough. But over the months that followed I began the painful journey to where I am now. I began to express the grief which I'd bottled up for so long. I wrote a letter to Chris telling him how angry I was at what he'd done to me and read it out loud to the counsellor. By the end I was crying, whispering, 'But I loved you.'

An old school friend began calling at my parents (Mum at work again I reckon!). She'd just got divorced and was still raw, so we made *a right cheerful pair. But we went out for a drink or a walk, and one night we even braved the cinema, and gradually, ever so gradually, I began to come to. I started a part-time job helping at a day centre for people with learning difficulties. They taught me so much. It was like they could feel how much I still hurt and gave me so much love.*

On the second anniversary of Chris' death I went, on my own, to the cemetery he'd been buried in. It was the first time I'd been. It was the city we met in and where Chris' parents still lived. I just sat at the grave side, cried quite a bit, and then started talking aloud to Chris, telling him about what I was doing and how sorry I was that I hadn't stopped him taking all those pills. At some point I realized that two people were standing close by. Our eyes met and then they slowly walked towards me. I cried again and just walked into their arms. It was Chris' parents, and for ages we just stood there holding each other, not saying a word.

Then the apologies started. Me for not having been in touch. Them for blaming me. It was like a scene from a weepie movie, but it was for real. I went back to their house and talked for hours about Chris. I told them things they'd never heard before and they told me about his childhood and how proud they'd been when he'd landed such a good job in the north. 'What a waste!' his dad said. And it was.

Those words went over and over in my head on the way back home. With a shock I realized I'd wasted quite a lot of my own life over the last two years. I was struck by how fragile life was and made a late New Year resolution that no matter how little or how much of it there was ahead of me, I was going to live life. And to the surprise of my parents I got home and took them out for dinner in the most expensive restaurant in the town. Just a small 'thank you' for the way they'd stood by me.

For Joan the sudden death of her husband was even more of a shock because they were young and because they had never even considered the possibility of death. That isn't always the case.

Gerald's story

Sylvia and Gerald had been married for thirty-nine years and had a number of what they used to term 'near misses'. Gerald had been seriously injured in a car accident, Sylvia had been successfully treated for cancer. Theirs was a fiery relationship, even after all the time they had spent together. It didn't take much for one or the other to start arguing if something wasn't quite right.

One day in April 1990 was one of those days. It was breakfast time and Gerald was annoyed because there was none of his usual breakfast cereal left. He complained vociferously and went stomping off to his workshop in the garden.

About eleven I ventured out to make amends, but there was no sign of Sylvia. Her coat and handbag had gone so I assumed she'd gone shopping. Not before time, I thought. I made a coffee and settled down to read the newspaper. By lunch-time there was still no sign of her and I began to feel uneasy. She wouldn't have walked out on me now, would she? Not after all this time!

And then the phone rang. It was a nursing Sister at the hospital saying my wife had been taken seriously ill while out shopping. She was in the accident and emergency unit and perhaps I could get over there as soon as possible. 'No!' I remember thinking. 'There has to be a mistake. My wife was well when she left this morning.'

I called a taxi and while waiting for it to arrive I paced the house. 'Please God, not Sylvia. I promise I'll never argue with her again, just don't let it be her.' In minutes I was at the hospital. The receptionist in the casualty area pointed to a seat. I refused. 'I've been asked to get here quickly to see my wife. I want to see her now. Will you please go and get someone in authority.' In my head I heard Sylvia's voice as she complained to her friend about me. 'Gerald can be so embarrassing sometimes. He even demands to see the manager in restaurants.'

The Sister who'd phoned me appeared, and we went into a small room nearby. I asked how Sylvia was. 'I'm sorry. She died ten minutes ago, just after I phoned. It was a massive heart attack.' I was so angry. I shouted at her for not phoning me sooner. I criticized the hospital for not being good enough and then I demanded to see the doctor who had treated her.

'Why couldn't you save her?' Gently and calmly the consultant explained that sometimes with heart attacks the damage is so great

70

that there is nothing at all they can do. He told me they had tried everything in their power but the damage was too great. Slowly I began to understand. But she'd had no heart problems; when they'd treated the bowel cancer, everyone had said what good shape she was in. The consultant was sympathetic. 'People who've never had a day's illness can suddenly suffer a fatal heart attack. It's uncommon, but it happens.'

It happens! It happens! The anger flared up again. It was my wife Sylvia he was talking about. The typical hospital cup of tea turned up then. 'We're sorry Sylvia's dead, but have a cup of tea instead.' The rhyme was in my head and wouldn't go away. I started to laugh, quite hysterically, and then I started to sob. No tears, but just great body-rattling sobs.

I lose track of time now. I called our two sons at some point and discovered one of them was on a business trip to New York and the other couldn't get here till late that night. And I tried to get hold of our vicar, but he was on the golf-course. It was all turning into a nightmare.

They asked if I'd like to see Sylvia. 'What on earth for?' I remember asking. The Sister persevered. 'Of course you might not want to, but some people do find it very helpful.' I looked long and hard at her. 'Young woman, what you've got to understand is that my wife and I rowed this morning. I stormed off, calling her a forgetful old woman, and I never even said goodbye.' I'll never forget what the Sister said then. 'Well perhaps now you can see her, tell her what you really think of her, and then you can say goodbye.' I began to cry. I did see Sylvia. She looked really peaceful, younger almost. And I talked to her, told her that I was a silly old fool and I hadn't meant what I said that morning.

I've never been the demonstrative type. When I was a boy and my father was killed in the Second World War I was told not to cry. He'd died for his country and I should be proud of him. And I was also told that I needed to be a man now and look after my mother. Chin up, old boy. I was only ten! Since then I've always kept a tight rein on my emotions. But sitting there beside Sylvia, the guard slipped. I felt such regret for the things I'd never told her. Important things like I loved her and really needed her. I just hope that wherever she was she could hear me. Why did I have to wait till she died before I could tell her how much she meant to me?

It's now eighteen months since Sylvia died. I realize how much I took her for granted. And when I think back, I just can't understand why she never left me. Then I think of how similar our backgrounds were. She'd never have divorced me, it wasn't done. So was she unhappy inside or did she really like the crotchety way we rubbed along?

After the shock with the bowel cancer, I realized then how much I'd miss her. But you forget, don't you? As soon as she was recovered from surgery I put it all behind me and things just returned to the way they'd been before.

The days are so long now. I just can't fill them. I'm sixty-four years old. I retired at sixty and the future just stretches bleakly ahead. My sons I see about twice a year, I play golf once a week, I go to church on Sunday, and that's it. The sum total of my life. Great, isn't it?

Sudden deaths such as Sylvia's often generate feelings of regret. Day by day we all take so much for granted, expecting tomorrow to be the same as today. And then when it isn't, the things we'd like to have said, the things we'd have liked to have done, become 'if only'. Yet it's all very well to say, 'Live each day as if your last!' It's easier said than done. And if we went around expecting everyone we loved to drop dead of a heart attack any minute, the nervous strain would be enormous.

The sadness for Gerald is that he still regrets so much. His childhood inculcation that big boys don't cry has shaped the rest of his life. It is only now, when he has lost someone who had been at his side for all his adult life, that he realizes how much of himself he hid away.

We could have done so much more. Travelling, the theatre, spending time with the children instead of sending them to boarding school. I look back now and ask myself what was it all for? We're born, we grow up, we marry, we have children, we work, we retire and then we die.

Yet nearly all my life I did what the 'oughts' told me. The good old stiff upper lip checking that I didn't enjoy myself too much, didn't feel too much. Sylvia's death taught me the futility of all that and I so wish that she were here to share the discovery with me.

Both of the accounts in this chapter reveal a lot of sadness and suffering. Both were heightened by the suddenness of the death. There was no time for any preparation, or any chance to tackle what is often called 'the unfinished business'. If Gerald had been able to have another twenty-four hours with Sylvia then he might well have been able to voice the things he'd always felt uncomfortable saying. If Joan had known that Chris would die, say in three months, then although she would still have had much grieving to do, those three months would have helped prepare her. It might also have meant that her relationship with Chris' parents was maintained throughout her grief.

But none of that was to be. Neither Sylvia nor Chris could have known much of what was happening to them, and it was the people closest to them who were the hardest hit. In circumstances where we are reeling from the intense bereavement of a sudden death is there anything we can do which might help?

The previous chapter describes the processes and stages of grief. It is possible, however, that some people will feel those stages much more intensely than others. Anger and disbelief are often more prominent in cases of sudden death. To lose someone with no warning and absolutely no chance of saying any kind of goodbye is deeply shocking. There can be enormous anger, sometimes directed at people we feel could have prevented the death. Disbelief, too, that the death happened at all. We pass someone in the street and think, for a split second, that it's the deceased person. The phone rings, a key turns in the lock and, sometimes months after the death, we can still think it's them. And none of that is surprising or strange. It all happened so quickly that one part of us still doesn't fully accept what has happened. It takes time.

One of the hardest things to handle with a sudden death is the area of regret. The things we wish we'd been able to say, the future we wish we'd been able to share. Some people find their level of regret is so great that it totally dominates their lives. In these circumstances a bereavement counsellor may encourage the writing of a letter to the person who died, just as Joan wrote, expressing all the things the bereaved person wishes they'd been able to say. Or they might ask: 'Imagine the person you're grieving for is sitting in that empty chair opposite you—what is it you want to say to them?'

These are useful devices to help put into words some of that terrible regret which, at the moment, feels like a heavy load. Nobody promises that it will take away the pain, but it is helpful to identify just what the areas of regret are, perhaps because some of them might turn out to be completely unrealistic. It's no good wishing a relationship had been perfect. Relationships are never perfect. We are, when all is said and done, fallible, sinful, and not always sensible human beings, and accepting this can help bring back a sense of proportion.

But if there's a particular incident we regret or feel guilty about, and we find we cannot get it out of our minds, we could try writing it all in a letter of apology. What should we do when the letter is written? We can post it to the counsellor, if there is one. Or we can take it to the graveside and read it aloud. Another possibility would be to burn it, thereby symbolizing that the incident is no more. People who are part of a Christian tradition which hears confession can find it helpful to confess formally and receive absolution from a priest.

Alternatively, we can truly believe that through Jesus Christ our sins are forgiven and read again the account of Jesus and the woman accused of adultery (John 8:1–8). It's the story of how the scribes and the pharisees brought her to Jesus saying that the law of Moses stated that as an adultress she should be stoned. What did he think? He appears to ignore the question. But when pressed, he states, 'If any of you are without sin, then cast the first stone.' They all wander off, leaving the woman alone with Jesus. 'Has nobody condemned you?' he asks. 'No one!' 'Then neither do I. Go, and sin no more.' Imagine that instead of the woman in that story, it is you who is brought for condemnation for that incident you so regret. What is said about you? Who is condemning you? Maybe there is no one to condemn you but yourself? How do you feel? And then move on in the story, to the point where all the accusers have to admit that in some way they too are guilty. There is no one else who hasn't sinned either. And then Jesus says to you, 'Does no one condemn you? Then neither do I!' How does that feel? What do you want to say?

If you did the exercise but still feel driven by guilt it is important to understand why you may be hanging on to that guilt. It sounds an odd thing to say that people hang on to their guilt. But it may be a way of punishing ourselves, or of preventing us from feeling other equally strong emotions. As long as we continue to cling to the guilt, we affect the way we feel about the future, too. It can prevent us from moving on, from adjusting to the life we must live without the person who died.

For a Christian, too, to continue living with a feeling of condemnation is to deny the reality of the gospel. No matter how awful we might have been, the forgiveness is there. To be really blunt, what is so special about any one of us that we feel we can never be forgiven?

These are tough words, but they are not meant to be unkind—on the contrary. Real kindness to ourselves means facing guilt square on, looking it full in the face, and accepting that it can go. If we have the strength to live daily with guilt then we also have the strength to live without it.

It is also important to understand that we may need the help of a professional counsellor to help find the root cause of persistent guilt. There is no shame or stigma attached to seeking such help, and many people have found that counselling has helped them to gain valuable insight into why they feel as they do.

One of the most tragic instances of sudden death is cot-death, or Sudden Infant Death Syndrome (SIDS) as it is also known. It is acknowledged amongst new mothers as one of their biggest fears and, as so little is known about its cause, there is little to be done to avoid it. A baby can be put to bed one night looking perfectly healthy, and then found the next morning, dead.

Nicola and Jack's story

The sad event of sudden infant death is exactly what happened to Nicola and her husband, Jack. Their son, Gavin, was four months old on the day he was found dead. They had two older children—Timothy aged five and Sally aged three.

G avin had always been a healthy baby, despite the fact he was born three weeks prematurely. He had a huge appetite and sometimes I felt guilty that I didn't seem to be enough for him. Jack used to pull my leg when I said this, telling me that I was getting on a bit now, and that made a difference.

The day before he died had been a good one. We'd gone for a family picnic on a warm, early spring day. Everyone had been in a good mood and it was good to be together as a family. We'd brought the children back tired and happy, and all went off to bed with no trouble at all. Jack and I enjoyed the peace and quiet until about midnight when Gavin woke up demanding to be fed. He wasn't quite as hungry as usual, but I didn't think anything of it.

It was 5.35 the next morning when I woke with a start, feeling terribly uneasy. The house seemed unnaturally quiet and I felt compelled to check that the children were all right. Timothy and Sally were sound asleep. But as I stood outside Gavin's door, I had a really strong sense of what I would find. And I did. He was lying face down, so still, and I knew he was dead.

I picked him up. There was no point in trying to recuscitate him. He had been dead some time, I guessed. I sat on the floor in his room, rocking him gently from side to side. I stroked his hair. I wrapped him up to keep him warm. We sat there together, me and Gavin, in what felt like the timelessness of eternity. I didn't cry. I kept watch in case, somehow, my son needed me.

Jack came. He took in the scene and knew immediately. He cried, and then I did too. Now I knew my link with Gavin had gone. A doctor came. The police came. My baby was going to be taken from me. What were we to tell Timothy and Sally who, through all of this, were downstairs watching videos, quieter than I can ever remember?

We told them together. We said that Gavin had died, just like Granny had last year, and that he had gone to heaven. Sally wanted to know why, if he was in heaven, the doctor had come to look at him. So we asked if they would like to see Gavin and say goodbye to him, because he was soon to be taken to hospital to find out why he had died. (As I said those words, I prayed they wouldn't ask how. They didn't; they were more interested in seeing Gavin.)

When they came to take Gavin for the post-mortem there we all were in the lounge. The children had each held him. Sally was quite matter-of-fact about the whole thing, wanting to know if he would be buried in the garden with Fergus, the cat, who'd died just last month. Timothy was more upset. When we'd told him I was expecting a baby, he'd said he wanted a brother. And now he understood that his brother had gone.

One of the worst moments was when we had to go and register his death, once his tiny body had undergone the post-mortem. It was such a short time since we'd been there proudly registering his birth. As I watched the pen recording the end of my dear son's life, I couldn't believe this was happening to us. It all seemed so unreal. Was Gavin really dead? Was this all just a nightmare that I'd wake up from? Yet inside me a deep, deep ache, coupled with a feeling akin to terror, told me it was all so horribly true.

There was a funeral, a very simple one. Jack carried the tiny white coffin into the chapel and I couldn't help but remember the day that Jack had so cheerfully carried Gavin from the car to home, shortly after his birth. And now, less than four months later our son was dead, and the post-mortem had revealed no reason for it. Inside I felt so angry I thought I'd explode. How can a perfectly healthy baby just die?

People said how wonderful we were. And then we were expected to get back to normal. Normal? What's normal when one day your life revolves around a demanding infant, and the next there's nothing more you can do for him? He's gone.

My breasts ached and leaked with the milk I couldn't give my son. I looked in the mirror and saw someone who wasn't fit to be a mother. She'd failed. She'd let her son die. And when Jack tried to cuddle me I shook him off. His touch was a reminder of the love which had conceived Gavin and which I was no longer worthy of.

Three months later I still hated my body. I wouldn't let Jack near me. I was terrified something would happen to Timothy and Sally and would never rest when they were out of my sight. One night Jack erupted. 'You're not the only one who's lost a son, you know. I really feel for you, but he was my son too. It was a shock, but it was three months ago and since then you've shut me out. I don't know what you're thinking. I don't know what's going on in your head. I can't bear the way you freeze when I touch you—like I'm a murderer. Tell me if you think I'm to blame for Gavin's death!'

I remember staring at him. He thought he was to blame, but it was *my fault, my body which hadn't been enough for Gavin. I was the murderer. And with that we started to talk and we talked long into the night. We rediscovered our love for one another.*

The next day we made an appointment to see our GP together. Helpfully she explained again what we already knew but couldn't believe. That it wasn't our fault Gavin had died. The room may have been too hot or too cold; it might have been better if he'd been put to bed, lying on his back, but then the other two had survived sleeping on their sides hadn't they? Finally I think we were both reassured. There was no real reason why Gavin had died. It seems he took a breath and then, quite simply, forgot to take another. And no one can be to blame for that.

Guilt, anger, panic, anxiety, disbelief, confusion. They are all emotions that can turn us upside down and inside out. The world begins to feel like an unsafe place with all manner of horrors just waiting round the corner to get us. The protective adult coat we wear which is woven from confidence and experience is ripped from us, and beneath is the vulnerable child: unsure, ill-prepared, fearful. This is what bereavement can do to us, and it is more likely to do it when a death has been sudden and completely unexpected.

And then one day, we realize things have shifted almost imperceptibly. One day we may feel OK, the next may be bad, but the OK times are getting longer. Through both the good and the bad we should treat ourselves gently. We must try not to deny the love which people around are offering; and if our grief is a grief they also share, we must also try not to shut them out.

Sudden death rips our world apart. It is profoundly shocking. Disbelief, anger, numbness, guilt become daily companions. And the question 'why?' keeps recurring. Sometimes that 'why?' can never be answered, and we can feel haunted by the fact that 'we never even said goodbye!' At times there can be no words which will comfort, no thoughts which will ease the agony of endless questioning. Our only chance of survival and sanity may be to accept the love of others and allow ourselves to express the agony which is tearing us apart inside.

6

'YOU CAN ALWAYS HAVE ANOTHER'
The hidden bereavements

I was thirty-two weeks pregnant when I began to worry that I couldn't feel the baby moving. The kicking had stopped. My GP said not to worry, there wasn't much room as the baby grew and they did get quieter. I wasn't satisfied and phoned up the hospital. They put me on a monitor, but they started to look worried. When the third doctor came in to try and find a heartbeat I asked, 'My baby's dead, isn't it?' He nodded, 'I'm sorry, but it looks that way!'

Our baby lived just ten hours. He was born four weeks early and when I heard the urgent, whispered voices of the medical staff as soon as I'd delivered him I was worried. He was rushed off to the Special Care Baby Unit, and they told us he was having difficulty breathing. Jack stayed with me for a time but went to find out what was happening. Just ten hours after he was born, our baby son died. They dressed him and wrapped him in a shawl and Jack and I were able to hold him, for the first and last time.

Each year in the United Kingdom some 7,000 babies will be stillborn or die shortly after birth. Sadly, these are so often the unacknowledged bereavements. They are due to miscarriage (the term used when a pregnancy is lost before twenty-four weeks), stillbirth, and neonatal death (a death which happens within twenty-eight days of birth). Parents who have suffered in this way report that medical staff, friends and relatives say things like, 'Never mind, you can always have another,' or 'Well it wasn't a real baby yet, don't upset yourself so much!'

Such clichés are probably said with the best of motives. Nonetheless, they ride rough-shod over the feelings of people who are grieving the loss of their baby. For the parents and particularly the mother, that fetus was their baby. It was wanted, it was being planned for, and then—it's gone.

Part of the problem seems to be one of language. Sometimes it seems as if the medical terminology—miscarriage, spontaneous abortion, the inviability of the fetus—disguises what the parents feel. To the father and mother, the simple fact is that their much-anticipated baby is dead. It is likely that they will have seen the moving image of their baby on a scan and, from that moment on, the pregnancy will have been a reality: a baby is on the way. They may well have been reading the baby books which tell you when the different organs form or what the likely sizes of the fingers and toes are. They could well have begun to think about names and, if it is a first child, begun to day-dream about what it would be like to have a child in the house.

And then, suddenly, it is all over. The woman is no longer pregnant. For some reason, and nobody may know why, she miscarried. There is nothing to show for the pregnancy, that morning sickness was all in vain, and she feels tearful and sad. 'Sudden change in hormone levels,' she might be told, but it is more than that. She is grieving her unborn child.

Suzanne and Graham's story

Suzanne worked as a teacher at the local comprehensive. She had been there for ten years. Graham, her husband, was a sales representative for a large company and spent a lot of time away from home, travelling the length and breadth of the country. Two years previously they had decided it was time to start a family and despite knowing the statistics, expected immediate success. A year later there was still no sign of a pregnancy and they consulted their GP. She advised them to relax and, much to their embarrassment, checked that they knew the basic facts of life. She said to give it another year before being referred for infertility investigations. Suzanne, now thirty-two, didn't want to wait. She wanted to find out now if there was a problem, but the GP insisted. Another six months to let nature take its course.

Six months later there was still no pregnancy. This time the GP agreed to refer them, adding that the waiting list for first appointments was about a year. Suzanne exploded. Didn't the doctor realize how much they wanted a baby? The GP had shrugged unsympathetically.

Suzanne and Graham began some research and, by going privately, received an appointment for one of the top infertility clinics in the country. Suzanne realized how sensitive she had become. She had become easily upset by television advertisements which featured mums and bright, smiling children, or by the number of prams in the high street, or again by casual questions from people at church—'No children yet?' It all rankled. Suzanne was also conscious of how the calendar now ruled their lives. Graham planned his work around being able to get home for that critical time mid-cycle, and their lovemaking was turning into a chore.

Suzanne grins.

*I*f I'd thought it was bad then, it was much worse once we'd been along to the clinic. Temperature charts, sperm counts and a whole barrage of tests for me. Some were quite painful, but at the end of it all we knew that there was physically no apparent reason why I was unable to conceive.

During all this time, apart from me telling my best friend about it, we didn't breathe a word to anyone. At work I pleaded an upset stomach if I had to take a day off to keep an appointment. We had just had an appointment with the consultant where he had talked through the various types of assisted conception available to us and we had said we'd go away and talk about it together, when I realized I might just be pregnant.

Maybe it was stress that was making me late, I thought. But after four days I couldn't wait any longer and went to the chemist to buy a home pregnancy test. I raced home from school knowing that Graham wouldn't be back for at least another two hours, and disappeared into the bathroom to do the necessary.

One hour later I knew. This was it. I was finally pregnant. Alleluia! I'd been beginning to think that God never intended us to be parents, but no, here was the proof. Graham was as over the moon as I was.

I kept on working, even with the morning sickness, and I tried to keep it quiet that I was pregnant. But I was so happy that people kept asking me if I'd won the pools or something. So, when I was eight weeks, I told them. Graham's and my parents were thrilled. It would be their first grandchild. A couple of the old dears at church told me they were glad we hadn't waited any longer. If only they knew!

My colleagues at work were pleased for us because I think my happiness showed how much this baby was wanted and I really knew the secret was out when one of my First Years piped up in class with, 'Please, Miss, is it true you're going to have a baby?' 'Yes,' I said with a cheesy grin, forgiving her impertinence, 'I'm going to have a baby.'

Whenever I'd read the baby books I always skipped the chapter on miscarriage. It had taken so long to get to this stage, I couldn't believe God would let me lose it. My mind was completely closed to the possibility. So when, at sixteen weeks, I started bleeding slightly, I didn't say anything—not even to Graham. I couldn't bear to worry him. It couldn't be anything to be concerned about, surely?

Famous last words. Two days later, just after we finished tea, I felt a sharp cramp, and then another, and within half an hour I was in a lot of pain. Graham called out a doctor who got me straight into hospital. For the next two days, the bleeding got worse and then eased, the pain increased and then almost stopped. A scan showed that the baby's heart was still beating. I began to feel optimistic, but then at 3 a.m. I began to get terrible cramps and the bleeding began again.

I lay in bed pleading with God to stop what was happening. My tiny, tiny baby wasn't ready to be born. But as the pains kept coming, I felt despair. My prayers were unheard. Through the pain I could feel only desolation and the most awful loneliness. No one could comfort me. The labour that should have brought the child of my dreams was killing my baby, expelling it violently into the outside world.

Afterwards the midwife told me I'd been carrying a girl, but I didn't want to look and so now when I think about it, I'm still haunted by the thought that our baby girl had been hideously deformed. The doctor I asked later said that the baby had been normal, but a bit of me still can't believe that.

I can't describe how I felt, not properly. When Graham arrived, once it was all over, I couldn't talk to him. I was both angry with him that he hadn't been there for me and, at the same time, guilty that I'd 'lost' the baby we both had wanted so much. Obviously he was upset, but he tried to hide it all by being matter-of-fact and practical. That made me even more angry with him.

As I left the ward one of the nurses came up to me, touched my arm and whispered, 'I know how you're feeling. I lost my first too, but I've got two healthy kids now.' I just nodded, but inside I was resentful. She couldn't know how I was feeling. I didn't want any other baby. I wanted the one I'd just lost.

Back at home I couldn't settle. I kept asking God why, and then I began to feel guilty. Maybe it was my fault. Maybe I should have stopped working and rested more, maybe it was something I'd eaten. Maybe, deep down, I didn't really want a baby. That was why I couldn't get pregnant, that's why I lost it. Ridiculous, I know, but all these thoughts kept coming.

One of the worst bits was coping with other people. Our parents tried to be supportive, but I sensed how upset they were inside. I found myself feeling guilty that I'd failed to give them a grandchild. Then, at work, I felt a failure. I felt the kids were thinking that I couldn't even have a baby let alone teach them properly. Silly really, but it's how I felt!

I was so tearful and really tired. It was like I'd lost all my energy and it was a real struggle to do anything. I got up in the morning, drove to school, did what I had to do, and then came home and went to bed. Graham started to get annoyed with me. He'd been really great to begin with, but he thought I ought to be over it by now and wanted to try for another baby. Seems he'd fallen for the popular myth that it's as well to get pregnant as soon as possible. The 'you can always have another one' school of thought. Had he forgotten how difficult it had been to have the first one?

We'd so wanted that baby. Every month when I found I wasn't pregnant had been such a disappointment. We'd spent a lot of money, too, trying to find out why we couldn't conceive. We'd have been good parents, I kept thinking, resentful of the newspaper accounts which told of babies being battered, abortion figures, and teenage pregnancy rates.

Two months after the miscarriage, one of the women from church, Maureen, who I knew by sight but had never really spoken to before, asked if she could come round for coffee one evening. She said she'd had four miscarriages and wondered if I'd like to talk. I wasn't sure I could bear her story but it seemed impolite to refuse. And deep down, I realized I wanted to know how Maureen felt about it all.

I'll never forget the evening she came round. It was so helpful. Maureen encouraged me to talk by sharing some of what she felt, and I found I was able to tell her things that I hadn't even shared with Graham. She talked of the need to mourn, just as I would if I'd lost anyone else I loved and told me how, after she lost her fourth pregnancy, she'd had a short funeral service in the hospital chapel. That amazed me. It never occurred to me that you might have a funeral service for a miscarriage, but thinking about it, it made sense. After all, it was the loss of a human life even if it wasn't fully formed yet.

Suzanne now looks back on that evening as a turning point. Realizing that she felt so awful because she was bereaved helped enormously. She wasn't abnormal. If anyone was abnormal, it was the people who thought she ought not to be feeling such a loss.

Two years later Suzanne conceived again. Despite the anxiety that she felt right the way through this pregnancy, she gave birth to a healthy baby boy.

Pregnancy is the growth of new life. The desire to have children, to create the next generation, is essential to the future of the human race. It is an instinct that runs deep, and perhaps again it is the technological sophistication of developed cultures which makes miscarriage 'a hidden bereavement'. Birth control and life expectancy lead us to believe that we can have children when we want and they will live to a grand old age. In the poorer Third World countries, life and death are much closer to everyone's experience. People there are painfully conscious that they are not in control of their own destiny and are only too aware of the unpredictability of life.

But here, in the West, we like to think that we are in control. Medical science has led us to expect so much. Suzanne, and many women in similar situations, have so much of their future pinned on the unborn child: hopes, dreams, the beginning of a new family unit. Yet when they lose all of that future with the death of their baby, their loss, if not unrecognized, is often dismissed or devalued. The lack of recognition of miscarriage as a bereavement denies a woman the chance to mourn. As we saw in chapter three, unexpressed and unrecognized grief can be destructive to health and to relationships.

The church has only very recently recognized that parents might appreciate the opportunity to hold a simple religious service in memory of a new life lost prematurely. There are now simple orders of service that are available for parents who would like to use them. Moreover, some hospital chaplains hold annual services for parents who have lost their babies through termination, spontaneous abortion, miscarriage, stillbirth or neonatal death.

One of the most moving research interviews I recall from my twelve years in broadcasting was with a woman in her fifties. At the age of twenty she had given birth to a stillborn baby in the twenty-seventh week of pregnancy. Her eyes filled with tears as she described how she felt about that event. Seemingly she never saw the baby, it was taken away. When she asked if it was a boy or a girl she was told not even to think about it. The baby was dead and it would be better if she forgot it. Since then, she said, she had been haunted by the memory. Perhaps the child had been hideously deformed, and although she went on to have other, healthy children, she said she always wondered.

It is hard to accept that what appears today as sheer callousness was the perceived wisdom of that time. Yet it is still only very recently that mothers and fathers have been encouraged to hold their stillborn babies after delivery. SANDS (the Stillbirth and Neonatal Death Society) is a charitable organization which befriends parents who have lost babies. It has also been very active in persuading health authorities and health professionals to recognize the need for parents to have the opportunity to grieve.

To show just how much attitudes have changed, compare the following story with that of the woman whose baby was taken from her and whom she never saw.

Gail and Harry's story

Gail and Harry brought in the New Year of 1991 toasting the health of their unborn baby. It had been a straightforward first pregnancy and in just ten weeks' time they would be parents. Just a few days after their celebration Gail went along for a routine check-up and was admitted to hospital immediately. Two hours later they told her the baby was dead.

*H*arry was with me by then, but neither of us could say anything. We were so completely shocked. The doctor said that the baby had died in my womb, but they didn't know why. He was very gentle and really sympathetic and not at all embarrassed by the fact that both Harry and I were crying. He said he'd leave us alone for a few minutes but then he'd be back to set up a drip which would send me into labour.

Labour! The pain all my friends told me was bearable because you knew you were going to get a baby at the end of it. I had to go through it, knowing that I was going to deliver a dead child at the end of it all. My body, the incubator of new life, was now a coffin.

Those twelve hours have to be the worst of my life, despite the painkilling drugs I received. They may have eased the physical pain, but nothing could touch the mental anguish. It was like time stood still and we were to be frozen in despair for eternity. There was to be no end to the torture, and we were to endure it on our own. Harry felt that way too. We cried a lot and he held me.

When our baby boy was eventually born, the midwife cried too. After a few minutes she went to hand him to me, but I didn't want to look. Harry did, though, and cradling our son in his arms he said, 'Look at him, Gail, he's so small and perfect.' 'And dead!' I added. But I reached for the bundle and found myself looking at our son's tiny form. I touched his minute fingers, felt the softness of the palm of his hands. We were left in peace for a while. I've no idea how long, but together we cried for our dead son and we decided to call him William.

Harry comes from a church-going family, and he wanted William to be blessed by the chaplain. It was a simple ceremony. I held William in my arms, and Harry held me. The words the chaplain used just washed over me, but afterwards I felt calmer, and it felt as if we'd done something good for William.

I stayed in hospital that night but left the next morning, never seeing William again. As we left I was given a leaflet produced by SANDS and the midwife who had delivered William gave me some photographs of him, a lock of his thin wispy hair, a copy of his hand and feet prints, and an identity bracelet with the date on it and his weight—3lbs 2 ozs. We were also given a certificate of stillbirth which we had to take to the registrar's office within six weeks.

We really treasure those few things as they are all we have of our son. That's the tragedy of stillbirth. You carry a baby inside you for weeks and months, you plan for its future and then—nothing. No memories, no time together. That's why now, thinking back, it was so good to have the opportunity to see and hold William. He was so beautiful, looked so peaceful, like he was just sleeping. And then, of course, we had to leave the hospital without him. Driving away, with empty arms, was heart-breaking.

When I got home I went straight to the room we had been preparing for him and went round touching everything. The cot, the blankets, the clothes. Harry and I did nothing but cling to one another and cried until we could cry no more. That night I picked up the first jacket I had bought in readiness for William and took it to bed with me, resting my cheek on it.

Before all this happened I'd never had much time for religion, but now I found myself wondering if there really was a God. Might it be true that our son William was in some kind of heaven, whatever that means? I was torn between wanting to believe there was some kind of sense to this, and opting for a fatalistic acceptance that it was 'just one of those things'. Even now I'm not sure what I really believe. But about a month after I was home from hospital, still feeling incredibly upset and angry, I wanted to know what had happened to William's body. The hospital had said they would take care of all that for us, as we'd *both said we would leave it to them. But now I wanted to know.*

The best bet seemed to contact the hospital chaplain. He was so good, inviting me over to talk, but saying that if I felt that I couldn't go back into the hospital, he would meet me elsewhere. But I wanted to go back. I wanted to remind myself that I really had gone through that horrific experience and walking back through the doors of the hospital seemed to be one way of doing that. We met the next day, just him and me. (Harry was back at work and thought I was a bit mad to want to know where William was!)

The chaplain asked me how I was faring. At first I began with a noncommittal 'OK' but when he asked me why I wanted to know where William's body was, out it came. The anger, the resentment at friends who wouldn't talk with me about it, the guilt that in some way I'd killed my own baby, and now my dread that he'd ended up in a hospital incinerator! On that count he was able to reassure me. All the stillborn babies were buried at the nearby cemetery, together, and that there was a memorial stone which stated 'Never forgotten. We miss you all.'

He told me the story of the memorial stone. It wasn't there three years ago, just a corner of the cemetery, somewhat unkempt, with a few handmade wooden crosses. But a group of parents decided their babies should not be dismissed like this and approached the local council who had been quite willing to do something. The result was a memorial stone, and since then the same parents had given the hospital a Book of Remembrance in which parents could record their baby's name and have an inscription written.

The relief I felt, I can't tell you! Here were people who were not prepared to have their babies ignored, people who'd wanted to know where their babies were. I wasn't unhinged.

Gail and Harry went to visit the cemetery. They had William's name entered in the Book of Remembrance, and Gail started to attend the monthly meeting of SANDS where, by meeting with other people who had been through a similar experience, she was gradually able to come to terms with William's death. One year later she and Harry were expecting their second child.

This new baby will not be a replacement for William. He will always be our first-born and when his new brother or sister is old enough to understand then we will let them know that they had an elder brother who died. What I still find very hurtful, though, is that people—friends and relatives—won't talk about what's happened to us. It's like they just don't care, which I'm sure isn't true. I seem to have lost a few of my friends through it, but through the monthly meeting I went to for a time I made some very good friendships. It's something quite awful that we have in common, but it's a tremendous support. And now I'm involved in fund-raising for research with the hope that, in the future, what happened to me won't happen to anyone else.

The hidden bereavement of miscarriage, termination, stillbirth or neonatal death is only gradually being recognized. Sadly, it has taken the voices of the bereaved parents to instigate a greater acceptance of their loss. And, even now, there are still acounts of unfeeling behaviour on the part of professionals: the hospital chaplain who refused to hold a funeral service when asked by a distraught mother, saying that as the baby had been born before twenty-eight weeks there was no need; the doctor who said of an abnormal baby that it was just as well it had died, leaving the parents feeling that they were wrong to mourn.

Grief is nearly always a very lonely and isolating experience and it seems to be even more so in the circumstance of miscarriage or stillbirth. Other than the medical staff there is usually no one else who has shared the experience of the loss. Grandparents and children lose the hope and expectation of a new addition to the family (and in no way do I want to detract from the disappointment and bewilderment they may feel), but it is the parents who uniquely experience the loss of the new life they were expecting. In the circumstance of stillbirth or late miscarriage they are the ones with the tangible proof—their lifeless child.

The overwhelming sense of grief is probably heightened even further if, as is likely, this is the first major bereavement that the parents have encountered.

As well as the inevitable overwhelming sadness, there will also be other, deeply undermining, feelings. The greatest of these is guilt—'I'm a parent. I should have protected my unborn child.' Then there will be anger—'The doctors and midwives should have taken more care. They should have known something was wrong and prevented it.' There will be a dreadful sense of failure—'Healthy babies are born every day. I couldn't even manage that!' Lastly, there will be jealousy. 'Why's she got a healthy baby and I haven't?'

These are all powerful feelings and they can last for a long time, certainly more than a matter of weeks or months. Sadly, they can prove to be some of the most destructive feelings. Of those whose first baby has died, a large proportion separate within the following twelve months.

Even for those who are well supported and whose relationship is not threatened, the grief is always there to some degree.

One bad time for women whose babies died prematurely is the week of the original 'due date'. Anticipated at first as such a happy week, it is now simply to be endured. Other parents who shared antenatal classes or appointments are now showing their healthy newborn baby to the world. The pain when one of them asks, 'And what did you have?' is indescribable.

Anniversaries can also be particularly poignant. On the day they would have been singing 'Happy Birthday' to their three- or four- or eight-year old, parents recall instead the time that their baby died. Sometimes, on would-be birthdays, at Christmas, or anniversaries of the death, parents will do something special to mark the day. It might be as simple as lighting a candle, or walking together in a significant place. Whatever the action is, it is something the parents, and even the siblings, find valuable. It is a way of saying we have not forgotten our baby who died.

The key aspect of all these particular types of 'hidden' bereavement is the need people have to acknowledge that there was a baby who was much wanted. That is why funeral or memorial services, no matter how long after the death, can be helpful. A funeral service for a lost baby is a very sad event. It is harrowing for the parents and yet, at the same time, it helps them begin to take in the reality of their loss. Seeing the little coffin may be the first time they really take in that their baby did die. It was not a nightmare that they will soon wake up from, it is something dreadful which did occur and which they have to learn to live with.

Parents who did not have some kind of funeral service, particularly those whose babies died some years ago when attitudes were not so enlightened, often suffer from not having a focus for their grief. In some way they feel as if they are left in limbo, as if the event has not yet finished. Sometimes years afterwards they find themselves wondering what happened to their baby, feeling that, in some way, they should have marked their child's existence. Such people can be said to be stuck in their grieving but may, even now, be able to do something about it.

Hospital records (albeit only recent ones) may have photographs of the baby. Some hospitals do this as a matter of course, just in case parents later ask for them. But in whatever year the baby was lost, if it was agreed that the hospital would take care of arrangements, it is usually possible to get in touch and ask what happened. It is common that a hospital will have an arrangement with a local cemetery or crematorium and enquiries there should help find the baby's resting place. It may be a communal plot or memorial stone, but it is nonetheless a place which could be visited, if that is what is wanted.

Sometimes, five, ten, even twenty years after a stillbirth or late miscarriage, parents have found it useful to have a short service of remembrance for the baby they lost. Through all of that time, it may be that they haven't quite completed their grieving. The service of remembrance is an opportunity for them to finally acknowledge the loss and, through that, experience some healing of their grief.

Lesley and Bob's story

Lesley had a stillbirth in 1979. She was ill after the birth and was given no opportunity to see her son. All arrangements were left to the hospital, and she returned home stunned to find that the whole episode was greeted with silence. Friends, relatives and neighbours avoided any talk of what had happened. Her grief was never allowed expression.

Twelve years later, suffering from depression, she realized she was still mourning for her son. She visited the hospital where he was born and, by sympathetic staff, was shown the records relating to the birth. She was also told about the memorial services which were held in the chapel and was determined to attend the next one with her husband, Bob.

A s we arrived I was handed a card and, if I wanted, could write in my son's name and the day he died. This was then placed in a basket with cards from the other parents. The service began with the twenty-third psalm, there was a short reading and a few prayers—all very simple but expressing the pain felt by parents with the commendation of their babies to God's love. Then the basket with all the cards inside it was placed on the altar, a symbol of our committing our children to God's care.

There were lots of tears, of course, but for Bob and me they were healing tears. We were finally acknowledging our grief for our son's non-life. It had been twelve long, unfulfilling years. At last, the emptiness left me.

For parents who believe God is the source of all life and has a plan for their lives, a miscarriage or stillbirth can rock the foundations of that belief. Why would God allow them to conceive, plan for their child's future, and then have it taken away so suddenly and cruelly? This is especially so if the doctors or the post-mortem can reveal no reason whatsoever for the baby's death.

This was a key issue for Suzanne, whose story was recounted early in this chapter. There appeared to be no earthly reason for her pregnancy to end.

I just couldn't accept that God had willed this to happen. He knew how much we wanted that baby. He couldn't have taken it from us just to teach us a lesson! To me it seems almost blasphemous to say it was God's will. What sort of God would do that? If I'd been ill then there might have been a reason. If the baby had been deformed then again God might have had a reason. But there was no reason. I was healthy, and the baby had been progressing normally.

And then I start wondering if my baby had a soul, and was it now in heaven? And if so, and my baby was with God, what was the point of never having lived on earth? I've always believed that life is a gift which allows us to grow and develop, emotionally and spiritually, but my baby had no chance of that.

The questions went round and round. Why, why, why? Finally I had to confess I just did not know, and never would. But what I'm confident about is that God shared in our distress and our anger, he didn't cause it. As a couple and as individuals I can now say that we have grown through the loss of our baby, but I do not believe the miscarriage happened just to make us maturer and more loving to other people. That's just been the result.

The following words are taken from the beginning of the Church of Scotland's 'Funeral Service for a Stillborn Child' and they are the most appropriate way to end this chapter.

W e gather here on what is for all of us a very sad occasion. We were looking forward to a time of joy and happiness, and now there are tears and grief. We are left with a feeling of emptiness. All that has happened seems futile and pointless. Our minds are filled with questions to which there appear to be no answers. And we are left feeling lost: so many things we do not know; so many things we do not understand.

But there are some truths we do know. We know that the God who made us, loves us; that he loves us always; that, through his Son Jesus Christ, he has promised never to leave nor forsake us. And we know also that others before us have found that his strength is available for us, especially at those times when we feel we have no strength of our own.

7

'IF ONLY IT HAD BEEN ME INSTEAD!'
The death of a child

Our seven-year-old daughter was knocked down by a drunken driver. She spent four days in hospital on a life-support machine, but then died. That was three years ago, and I still cannot accept it. She had so much to live for, her future was all ahead of her.

I'm seventy-two years old and I never thought I'd have to cope with the death of one of my own children. Yet three months ago my youngest son died, aged forty. It's not right. He should have been burying me, not the other way round. I lost my husband just a year ago, but this is worse. My son had years more living to do, I haven't.

Our son was found to have a brain tumour. A year later he died, aged ten. We're a Christian family but I find it very hard to accept this was God's will. I read about other children being cured of their cancer, so why not my son? We learned so much from Ian and the way he coped with his illness but his death was still senseless.

The death of a child of any age seems wrong. It is against the natural order. Children are meant to bury their parents, not the other way round. The death of a child represents the death of so much unfulfilled potential, so many hopes for the future. In Victorian times families were large and child mortality was high; but today, with smaller families, a better standard of living and greater life expectancy, the death of a child is a rare and deeply shocking event. The experience of parents who have learned to live with the death of a child suggests that you never recover from it, you just learn to live better with it.

Karen and Hugh's story

Pat was eight when she first became ill. Her parents Karen and Hugh thought at first that it was a passing virus, but a week later Pat was still listless and Karen began to worry. The GP said there was a lot of 'it' going around and not to worry. When Pat still wasn't better a week later, Karen went back to the doctor. This time there were blood tests, and then a quick referral to a large teaching hospital in London.

When the paediatric consultant told us it was leukaemia, even though I'd been concerned about our quick referral to London, I just couldn't believe it. Pat couldn't be that ill. She didn't look that ill. Why, even that morning she'd been asking when she could go home. There had to be some mistake.

But there wasn't. I moved into special accommodation in the hospital to be close to Pat through the horrors of the next few weeks. When alone, I cried and cried when I thought what my daughter was going through. Endless blood tests, bone marrow tests, chemotherapy. Every time she had to have more tests I wanted to refuse. I hated the thought of what they were doing to her, and felt sick. It was my 'baby' they were doing it to. But Pat was so stoical through it all, even when her hair fell out. All she said about it was that it made her one of the gang! (There were three of them on the ward receiving chemo at the same time, and they were all quite matter-of-fact about it!)

The other children went into remission. Pat didn't. She died, quite suddenly, just two months after she was diagnosed. She'd slipped into a coma the previous evening and she died at two o'clock in the afternoon.

How to find the words to describe how I felt? Numb. Sick. Jealous of the parents whose children were now in remission. Angry. Looking back, it was like living on two levels. Outside I was the kind, loving mother successfully keeping her feelings under control; and inside I was being torn apart.

Before she died, Hugh and I sat with Pat all night and morning. We held her hand, talked to her, and I willed her to wake up. I remember praying endlessly, bargaining with God: 'Let Pat recover and I'll try so hard to be good for the rest of my life.'

And then the consultant told us that there was no hope of Pat pulling through. His words hit me as if he'd thrown icy water all over me. I couldn't breathe, and I felt as if I was going to faint. Up till then I'd believed she was going to be all right, no matter what Hugh and the doctors said to me. Now I had to realize my daughter was dying.

I went and sat on her bed, cradling her as much as I could. I could remember so vividly the day she was born—how frightened I was, but excited at the same time. Then so much joy and love when the midwife put her in my arms for the first time. It all seemed like yesterday, but now Pat was leaving me and nothing I could do would stop it. I couldn't cry, but the whole of my body was crying for me. My stomach cramped, my muscles ached, and there was a pain in my chest which went on for days.

Hugh and I talked to Pat. We told her she'd be safe and that her granny and grandad would be waiting for her when she was ready to go. Her breathing got slower, and as we told her how much we loved her, there came the inevitable moment when we realized it was all over. Pat had died, quietly and peacefully.

I remember standing at the window, looking down on the world outside. It all looked so normal. The sun was shining, there was a traffic jam, and people were walking purposefully around with briefcases and shopping bags. Across the road a young couple stood holding hands and gazing into each other's eyes. Young love! And that's when the tears began. Pat would never know what it's like to fall in love for the first time. She would never grow up; she would never be the airline pilot which she always used to tell people she wanted to be. What a complete and utter waste.

The staff on the ward were very kind and let us sit with Pat until we were ready to leave. A couple of the nurses who'd been Pat's favourites and the young doctor who'd spent a lot of time caring for her came in to say how sorry they were. My heart went out to them. There were so many really sick children on this ward, where did they get the emotional strength to keep on caring?

It was Hugh who suggested it was time for us to leave Pat. I couldn't bear to go. I didn't want her to be wheeled off to a mortuary as soon as we left but, after a bit longer, we did leave. I left Pat's favourite teddy lying next to her cheek and asked the Sister to make sure that Ted went with her. Sister agreed. I couldn't bear Pat to be completely on her own.

And then it was home to an empty house. It was so quiet. Peter, our five year old was staying with my sister, and now there was no Pat. Hugh and I just sat in the kitchen, staring into coffee mugs, trying to put off the moment when we had to tell everyone what had happened. We realized that once we'd done that, it was for real.

I just cannot describe those first few weeks adequately. Although I'd had time to think what might happen if Pat died, I'd never really thought she would. I'd met other parents on the ward whose children had been fighting leukaemia on and off for years, and had built a lot of hope on that. With Hugh I'd always talked about when Pat was better. We were going to go to Disneyland as a special treat.

Now I was torturing myself with what I'd done to Pat to give her leukaemia. Was it the food I'd given her? Or chemicals we'd used in the house? I would find myself sitting in her bedroom, which I just couldn't bear to change or do anything with, and would talk to her. I'd pick up her books, needing to touch something I knew she'd touched. It made me feel close to her.

You'd have thought Hugh and I would have been able to support one another through the pain we felt at Pat's death, but we barely talked. He went back to work soon and seemed to bury himself in his work. But I was at home all day and alone with my memories and thoughts. In the early days, soon after Pat's death, some of our friends had been really good, coming round for hours on end, letting us talk and cry and making sure we ate and that there was food in the house.

But, gradually, apart from Rose (an unmarried friend from school days), friends began to stop coming round. They'd phone occasionally to 'see if we were feeling better'. Anyone would think we'd just had flu, not lost a child! But Rose would come round in her lunch breaks, at least twice a week, and she'd let me talk about Pat. And when I cried she didn't get embarrassed or immediately look at her watch and say she had to leave!

I'm not sure we handled Peter as well as we might have. When Pat was ill in hospital, he'd been to see her. But when she'd taken a turn for the worse he'd gone to my sister so that we could both stay at the hospital. All we'd said at that time was that Pat was more poorly and we wanted to stay with her. He'd asked if he could come too, but we'd said it was better if he stayed with his auntie.

So, after Pat died, we didn't know what to tell him. He seemed too young to be told his big sister had died, so we decided to say that Pat had gone to live with Jesus and wouldn't be coming back. Peter didn't come to the funeral as I thought it would upset him, but a few weeks later Hugh was leaving for a four-day business trip and Peter became very upset. He wanted to know if Daddy was going off to live with Jesus too. So then I had to explain that Pat had died and in the end he came with me to her grave. We took flowers with us and he was really enthusiastic about doing that.

But two days later, when I discovered him in Pat's bedroom going through her toys and games, I exploded. I didn't want anyone to touch her things. When he said: 'But now Pat's dead, and with Jesus, she doesn't need them!' I dissolved, screamed at him for being heartless and sent him to bed while I howled in my own room. It hurts to tell that story because I sound like a monster. I suppose I was one, and I feel so guilty about doing it, but that's how I was then.

I know that I was so wrapped up in my own grief that I couldn't cope with how anyone else might feel. Emotionally I neglected Peter and I just thank God that he's as normal today as he is! As for Hugh I completely excluded him. He used to get impatient with me when he got back from work and found me in tears again. In turn I used to shout at him that he was abnormal. How could he be so matter-of-fact about his daughter's death?

The marriage between Karen and Hugh had virtually disintegrated by this time. It was six months after Pat's death and the grief was still very raw. But Rose, Karen's friend, was concerned and investigated what help might be available for Karen and Hugh. She phoned the local Social Services

Department and discovered a social worker who was a bereavement counsellor. The next step was to get Karen and Hugh to agree to see her. Much to Rose's surprise Hugh leapt at the opportunity—it was Karen who needed a bit of persuading. Let Hugh now explain why.

I knew we were in trouble. I couldn't get close to Karen. She was always crying and wouldn't let me touch her. I was feeling guilty that I'd failed as a father in letting Pat die. I'm meant to have protected her, and now I couldn't even comfort Karen. It was obvious we had to talk professionally with someone who didn't know us.

I was angry with Karen. She was wallowing around the place as if she was the only one who was grieving, but I was too. Men are brought up not to show their feelings, not to cry—they're taught to be strong. At work I could get my head down and ignore my pain. Anyway, somebody had to bring the money in, otherwise we'd have been homeless as well.

One of the good memories I've got from when Pat was in hospital was a week or so before she died. Karen was at round at her sister's with Peter, so it was just Pat and me on our own. She was very weak by this stage and couldn't really walk. She just looked straight at me and said: 'Daddy, I'm going to die, aren't I?'

How on earth do you tell your daughter that yes, she's dying? But I couldn't lie to her either. She was bright, she knew what had happened to one of the other children with leukaemia. So I took a deep breath and told her the truth as gently as I could. I held her hand as we talked, but then realized it was Pat who held my hand. My dying daughter was trying to comfort her father! She sighed and said, 'I hate being sick, Daddy. I don't even want to play any more. But when I go to heaven I'll be better.'

She paused and then went on, 'Mummy keeps telling me I'll get better. Don't tell her I know I'm going to die. She'll be ever so upset.' We hugged each other then, and I read to her before she fell asleep. Afterwards I didn't know what to do. Pat had been right. Karen refused to believe that Pat was going to die. The doctors had talked to us several times already, obviously trying to prepare us for Pat's death, but it was as if Karen couldn't hear what they said. I knew that when the inevitable happened Karen was going to take it very hard indeed.

But I didn't know how to prepare her.

That night I tried to talk to her about the prospect of Pat dying but she screamed at me, saying I'd given up hope. We had to will her to live! So I gave up. I had two more chats with Pat, on my own, before she slipped into a coma. I'll cherish those chats until my dying day. She knew what was happening and wasn't at all afraid. 'I'll just go to sleep and not wake up.' And the very last time, as I left she said, 'Tell Peter I'm sorry that I was so horrible to him. Bye-bye, Daddy. I love you.' I'm sure she knew that was the last time she'd see me.

My faith isn't very strong, but Pat taught me not to fear death. And what's more I now believe there is life after death and that Pat will be there waiting for me when I die. I've started going to church sometimes, but I can't get Karen to come with me. I tried to tell her about the conversations I'd had with Pat, but I think she feels guilty that she couldn't talk to Pat about it all.

Our marriage became a disaster. Karen and I couldn't communicate. People said, 'At least you've got each other.' That was a joke. We might have been living in the same house, but we hadn't 'got' each other. I wished we had. We needed each other. As for Peter, he'd not just lost his sister, his parents weren't up to much either.

Karen and Hugh did go to see a bereavement counsellor. They went together first of all and then separately. They also went to a support group. There they realized that other parents know what it was like to lose a child, and drew enormous support from that shared grief. Some months later Karen was able to see a difference in the way she felt.

I still miss Pat enormously, and it doesn't take much for me to cry, but I think our marriage has recovered. In counselling one day I had an image of Pat in my head and she was crying because her mummy and daddy were arguing. That had happened when she was about six, but suddenly I was thinking about what she would make of us now. And she would have been so upset.

I feel much closer to Hugh now. He's talked to me about Pat in her last few days and what she said; and he's right, I do feel guilty that I hadn't been able to talk to her about her death. But I'm glad he managed to talk to Pat, or rather, she was able to talk to him. It's also helped me to talk with other parents. There were times when I had, and still have, bizarre thoughts. Sometimes I think I'm going mad, but when you hear somebody else say the same thing you realize it's normal to feel like this when you've lost a child.

The group's also helped me think about how difficult it is for fathers when a child dies. All their upbringing is about being strong, and protecting their family. Their grief is just as real but they're brought up not to show it. I think that's worse. But my advice for any other couple going through the grief of losing a child is, whatever else you do, don't exclude one another. Let each other grieve in the way they need to, but share what you can. Now's the time you need one another.

Hugh and Karen are surviving together, but their story shows how easy it is for couples to be torn apart by the death of their child. The strongest of relationships can be tested by overwhelming grief. At the very time that you most need the other, you are so absorbed in your own grieving that it is easy for the non-communication, the alienation and the isolation to grow. Friends and colleagues find it difficult to know what to say, and bereavement brings powerful feelings that cut you off from other people. Wrapped in grief, the world outside seems a long way away—distant and removed. It's hard to hear what is said, and even more difficult to connect to it.

In the middle of such unaccustomed behaviour and reactions, it is worth struggling to hold on to one another. One woman described her relationship with her husband, after the death of a teenage son, as being 'shipwrecked'. Thrown into the raging sea on two flimsy bits of wood for security, they could just about link hands and support one another. But as the waves then broke around them, the fragile grip they had on one another slipped. 'Before we knew it, the currents of bereavement had parted us, and we couldn't even see or call to one another!'

For Christian parents the problems are no less burdensome. There may be additional guilt because we fear that our faith is not strong enough to see us through. There may be extra anger at God because we think he has taken our son or daughter. We rage at him for what he has allowed and we feel abandoned by him.

Ultimately it is best to be honest about what we think and feel. It is pointless to censor it in order to say what we think as Christians we ought to be say. It is far better to accept that we cannot make sense of our child's death. We can then share our confusion with God in our prayers, and even if our rage and anger make it impossible for us to pray with words God will nevertheless be with us. For it is in our deepest groans and cries, no matter how inarticulate and despairing we are, that we will find the Holy Spirit is at work. At the very bottom of the blackest pit, there is a rock on which to stand.

In our human thinking the death of any child seems a waste and senseless. There has been no time to develop into adulthood, no opportunity to enjoy all that the world has to offer. Learning to read, to question, to think independently—there's so much out there to discover. Is there any purpose to lives that are so short?

The answer has to be a resounding 'yes!' At one funeral service, a minister put a different thought to the mourners of an 18-month-old baby girl. For this child, he said, had lived a complete life. It had a beginning and a middle and an end. The span may have happened to be eighteen months, but it was a full lifespan, entire in itself. To grieve this loss deeply was right, and necessary. But to say that the child's life should be considered 'cut short' was to denegrate the fullness that was there and to minimize all the love and growth that existed for that time.

In fact, in this country some 12,000 children die every year. Are these children are special in any way? Are they purer souls than us, already spiritually mature enough to move on? Some parents would quite categorically say yes to these questions. Especially when illness has preceded a death, they feel that they have seen their child grow spiritually. In younger children this is seen more in the way they handle their illness than in any perception of what life might mean. But older children who understand the concept of their own death can show a wisdom and an acceptance which seems to go far beyond their years.

Geoff and Rachel's story

Geoff and Rachel are strong and active members of their local church. They had been unable to have a child of their own because Rachel had undergone a hysterectomy for endometriosis when she was just twenty-eight. As they had always wanted children they adopted Greg, when he was just a few weeks old. In no time at all Geoff and Rachel thought of Greg as their own son. They made no secret of the adoption, and Greg knew he was their special and much wanted son.

Greg was a sunny and happy child. He always wanted to know why. Why did birds fly, but people couldn't? Why wasn't it summer all the time? He liked to help people and once he'd joined the Cubs it became a family joke that he'd picked all the daffodils in the garden and sold them to his friends for Mothering Sunday. Then he'd given the proceeds to the local charity that the Cubs were supporting. Rachel had not been amused—well, at least not until the next day!

Time after time Geoff and Rachel thanked God for the gift of Greg. They marvelled at how full of life he was and how much joy he brought them. Never, back in those days when they had so desperately wanted a child, had they imagined it would be as good as this.

Greg talked quite naturally about God. He sang in the church choir and happily took part in daily family prayers. When he set out to Scouts, the evening after his eleventh birthday, he was his usual happy self. But thirty minutes later he was back. He said that he'd fallen off his bike when he'd braked suddenly to avoid a cat, and that he'd hit his head. He was white and very shaken.

Rachel decided to take him to the hospital's accident and emergency unit immediately. She was uneasy. She was even more alarmed when Greg said that he thought he was going to die and that she and Geoff musn't be too upset. 'Of course you're not!' was Rachel's response, but inside she was praying, 'Lord, don't let this be serious.'

The doctor up at the hospital was reassuring, but said they'd keep Greg in overnight for observation as he'd obviously taken a nasty knock to his head. Rachel and Geoff sat with him for an hour up on the ward but then Greg said he was fine and that they should go home and get some rest. As they left he kissed them both and thanked them for being the best parents in the world.

Rachel was completely unnerved by it and couldn't settle at all when she got home. She started to read her Bible, coming very quickly to Isaiah 43. 'Do not be afraid—I will save you. I have called you by name—you are mine. When you pass through deep waters, I will be with you; your troubles will not overwhelm you. When you pass through fire you will not be burnt; the hard trials that come will not hurt you. For I am the Lord your God.'

About midnight Geoff went to bed, but Rachel stayed up. It was a beautiful night outside, warm and tranquil and she took a rug out to the garden and sat there, sometimes praying for Greg's safety, sometimes just keeping a watchful vigil.

At 2.15 a.m. the phone rang. It was the Sister of the ward, asking them to come in. Greg had taken a turn for the worse and they might have to operate. At the hospital they learned that Greg was now unconscious and it was feared that he had internal bleeding in the skull. It needed immediate surgery to relieve the pressure on his brain. Rachel and Geoff were allowed just a few minutes with him, before he was wheeled off to theatre. Rachel said that she knew she would never see Greg alive again.

I felt so helpless. It was dreadful watching as they wheeled him away, knowing deep inside me that God was taking Greg to be with him. But as he went I sensed peace right through my body. I can't really describe it, but when the peace came I was able to pray inside me: 'Lord, not my will, but yours be done.'

Rachel's intuition was correct. Greg died on the operating table. When the Sister came into the room that Rachel and Geoff had been waiting in just after 4.30 a.m., Rachel was able to say, 'Greg died a short time ago didn't he? It's all over.'

Looking back over the year since Greg died, Rachel and Geoff firmly believe that they have grown closer together. This is part of the letter that they sent out with their Christmas cards, just six months after Greg's death.

Thank you for all the wonderful letters and cards you sent us after Greg's death. It was so comforting to know that you were praying for us in our sad loss and we want to tell you of how much we have felt upheld by God's love throughout our grief. Our mourning has not quite been turned into dancing—yet, but we are at least able to hear the music, and the feet are beginning to tap again!

We have spent the last six months trying to make sense of why Greg died. He had a bright future ahead of him and we loved him dearly. It was such an accidental death and we have asked ourselves endlessly if the hospital was negligent in not spotting that Greg had internal bleeding until it was too late. But none of that will bring Greg back. We have prayed and talked long and hard about the meaning of Greg's death and know only that we believe it was part of God's plan for Greg.

During his short life, Greg gave us so much love; and despite the pain of the last six months we don't for one moment regret adopting him over eleven years ago. Greg was the child we could never have and it's as if God loaned Greg to us, for us to love and care for him as we grew as parents.

This Christmas will be a sad one, our first without Greg. But as we quietly celebrate the gift of the Christ child to the world, pray for us that we can continue to thank God for his gift of Greg to us for those eleven short, but wonderful, years.

Rachel and Geoff's faith is remarkable. Their ability to thank God for Greg's short life in the midst of readily admitting they do not understand why his life was to be so short is a tribute to the place of faith. Their grief has been no less then anyone else's, and they would be the first to say that there have been some very dark days indeed. Faith should not be the spiritual tranquillizer of believers, because they too must mourn. Instead faith can enable us to believe that there is a time-scale in God's purpose, even if we cannot see it now.

Personally, I do not believe that God causes children to contract life-threatening and fatal illnesses, or to have accidents. Inasmuch as the world was created by God, and within it there are viruses and germs to which human beings can fall prey, then there may be a link. But if, as scientific research is beginning to show, it is the environmental damage caused by the human race which is leading to an increase in certain types of cancer, for instance, then whose 'fault' is that? God's or ours?

Arguments about accidental deaths are equally spurious. We

are not puppets with the strings of our lives pulled by a divine puppeteer, but human beings living on this planet within the laws of nature. If a three year old pulls free of her father and races into a road to investigate something that has caught her attention, and is fatally injured by a (man-made) car that happens to be passing at that particular moment, it is preposterous to me to say that God willed that child to run into the road.

Surely it was the personality and natural inquisitiveness of a three year old coupled with her inability to know the risk, that attracted her into the road? If there had been no car, then either her father might have joined her to look at the object in question or the child might have received a scolding, and that would have been that. If the car had been a second earlier or later, then again the child may have survived. But at that particular millisecond in time, in that particular sequence of events and people, the child was hit.

Of course, if it is impossible to accept that God willed it to happen, or didn't prevent it from happening, then the difficulty comes in living with the randomness of that particular set of circumstances. Are we really as prey to the effects of random action as we are to germs and viruses? Are we, to all intents and purposes, on our own in this accident-laden world?

To say we are on our own is too stark and simple. But we do have free will, whose consequence is freedom to make our own choices. There may well come a time when we, or someone we love, is in the wrong place at the wrong time and we have no option but to accept the result of that. It is not to say that God has no care for us, or no plan for us. We are simply subject to the natural laws of this world, and that is a part of the mystery of life.

Within this mystery, and freedom of choice, is the very essence of our humanity. Life is fragile and precious. We are not slaves to a tyrannical God who dictates our every move, but the children of a God who himself was born into this world as a vulnerable infant. God is not distant and remote, but there in our fragility and pain. In our raw vulnerability God hears and, above all, shares.

Is any of this of comfort to a parent who is grieving for a child? Life is not a simple puzzle. It is full of unanswerable questions, and that is where faith can be important. It may be impossible to make any real sense of a child's death. What we can believe is that the God of limitless love is right beside us, through all the pain and relentless slaughter of our emotions. Just as Mary wept at the foot of the cross, seeing her son's agonizing and humiliating death, so too we will weep. But as the months turn to years, some sense of perspective will return and in time, either in this world or the next, we will understand more fully the purposes of God.

8

TABOO DEATHS

Alcohol ruled my mother's life and killed her. Sometimes she managed to stop drinking. But the last time the doctors said if she drank again, that would be it—her liver would pack up. She was doing fine, but then she got made redundant and hit the booze. Six weeks later she was dead. People are all sympathetic when you say your mum's died. But when you say she drank herself to death their faces are a picture.

My brother was homosexual. My parents threw him out when he told them. I stayed in touch with him, though, and four years later I went to see him in London. He looked awful, really thin. That's when he told me, 'I've got AIDS, Jenny.' I left home too so I could be near him. Seven months later he died. I was with him and so was his partner, Ian.

My husband took his own life. I didn't even know there was anything wrong! The police told me they found his car with the engine running and the hose from my vacuum cleaner attached to the exhaust, running back into the car. He left a note. It didn't say much, just, 'Sorry. It's all got too much.' Now, when people ask me how my husband died, I just say it was a car accident.

Death is already a fairly unmentionable topic of conversation. The kinds of deaths described above are, however, even more taboo. People may offer sympathy to the newly bereaved, but there's definite censorship at any suggestion that the person might have been responsible for their own death. Of course, it's a nonsensical censorship: if a man dies because he was driving too fast, the recriminations are few, if any. More like a case of bad luck! But if the same man were deliberately to drive his car into a brick wall at fifty miles an hour then his death is likely to be regarded by friends and acquaintances in a distinctly unfavourable light. His immediate family can feel stigmatized and outcast. Yet both deaths are within the realm of personal responsibility—it is the lack of a will to live that society cannot accept.

This terrible duplicity about taboo deaths is all too evident today. Lung cancer as a direct result of smoking is all right; death from heroin addiction isn't. A heart attack is acceptable if it has been helped along by a lifetime of eating fats and by carrying an extra thirty kilos in weight; drinking oneself into liver failure is not. Why do we discriminate? A death, however it is caused, is a death. The people who were close, regardless of the cause, will grieve. Yet their grieving is made worse by being forced into even greater social isolation.

Angela's story

Angela and Tony were stalwart members of their local church. They lived in a beautiful little village in a picturesque part of the country. They had just one son, Roger. At eighteen he went up to university to study medicine. Angela was glad he'd decided to become a doctor as he was always very caring, even in early childhood. From time to time Tony had nagged, claiming Roger was too soft for his own good, and needed to toughen up. When the other boys in the village were out playing football, Roger preferred to read. But in his mother's eyes, it paid off. With three straight As at A-level he had the choice of the medical schools.

I missed him enormously when he went off to university, but he phoned every week and came back when he could. He seemed to enjoy university life. He got involved in the Christian Union and had no problems with his exams at all. Passes every time.

I always encouraged him to bring friends home with him. We have a large house with lots of space and I would love to have met his friends. But he never brought them. Tony used to quiz him about girlfriends, but he just said he was too busy. He was looking tired and strained now, but he said he was all right. That summer, before his second year, he announced he was going to work in Paris. He wanted to improve his French.

I was disappointed. I'd so looked forward to having him at home for three months, but I put on a brave face. He'd got to live his own life! But when he came back from Paris, he looked different. He was more confident and the slight stammer he'd had from childhood had gone.

That Christmas he asked if a friend called Martin might come to stay. He was a law student and his parents lived in Australia. It was too expensive for him to go back for Christmas. Well, I was delighted. Not just one, but two, boys to mother over Christmas. Martin was a lovely boy. Very good-looking, very polite and he often used to wander over to the church to play the organ. He was much better than our regular organist.

We had a lovely Christmas but then, on Boxing Day, we were invited to friends. Martin and Roger came too. Nothing untoward happened there, but on the way back Tony was really subdued. He said that he wanted to talk to Roger in private. Martin and I sat down in the kitchen with a mug of coffee. Soon I became aware of raised voices. Then Tony stormed in, ignored Martin, and announced he was going out. When he got back he hoped that Roger would have gone. Then Roger came in, and very calmly and lovingly told me he was gay and that he was in love with Martin. They both knew the church condemned homosexuality, but they couldn't deny how they felt.

I felt devastated. Not so much by what Roger had told me, but by the way his 'coming out' destroyed our family life. Tony was adamant that he never wanted to see or talk to Roger again. I never hid the fact that I remained in touch with Roger and managed to see him for an occasional weekend, but he never came back for Christmas or birthdays like he used to. It broke my heart that there was such a split.

We never told friends what had happened, just said that we'd drifted apart. I think inside me something died. I couldn't condemn my son. It wasn't what I'd have chosen for him, but he was a good young man. I couldn't see him as the pervert that Tony did. And as for Roger, he continued to do well at university and he and Martin started to live together.

Some years later Roger phoned me one day and asked if I'd visit, urgently. He sounded tense and distant, and I was worried.

It was then that the whole sad story emerged. A few months previously Martin had discovered he was HIV positive and now Roger was too. Just that day, after much thought, he had given up his career in medicine. The risk to his patients was infinitesimal, but he felt he couldn't hide his situation.

My heart broke for him. His sexuality had cost him his family and now it had cost him his career. I feared that it would soon cost him his life.

Four years later Martin died from AIDS and Roger began to show symptoms of the disease. He grieved deeply for Martin and I felt powerless to help him as he struggled with the loss of the man he loved. He received a lot of support from other gay friends, but he was bitter that Martin's parents (who'd come over from Australia) had forbidden him to attend Martin's funeral. I couldn't believe that anyone could be that callous, but Roger said such things were commonplace in the gay community. Several of his friends had undergone similar times of rejection.

Then, as Roger became sicker, he told me he was desperate to make his peace with his father. And, after all those years of turning his back on his son, Tony relented. Roger came home. I was delighted, but it was obvious he was now very ill. He was extremely thin, very uncertain on his feet, and the childhood stammer had come back. I could tell Tony was extremely shocked by the condition of his son. All of a sudden he began to cry, grabbed hold of Roger, and just held him close. 'Stay with us, son. We'll look after you. Get you fit and strong again!'

Roger looked straight at him and very softly said, 'Dad, I'll never be fit and well again. It's gone too far. It's just a matter of time. It might be weeks, it could be months. But that's all.' I've never seen Tony so out of control! He was in tears, berating himself for disowning his son, and asking forgiveness. And that's when father and son embraced, for the first time in seven long years.

Tony and I had to think about what to say to other people. We could say he had cancer. (Well in one sense, he did.) But to do that was to deny what Roger and all of us were living with. I felt there had been too much denial already and wanted people to know the truth. So that's what we did; and it was horrendous.

We discovered that many people have very judgmental attitudes to AIDS. Maybe it's because they are irrationally afraid it's catching; or because they condemn homosexuality. Whatever the reason, we realized we were on our own. Tony found that people who had been golfing partners for many a year were suddenly unavailable for a game. I walked into the local shop for some groceries and the shop fell silent and no one would meet my eye. My cleaning lady phoned to say that she was very sorry but she couldn't come any more. She didn't want to pass it on to any of her own family. Invitations to go out for dinner dried up, virtually overnight. Apart from one—Deidre, a dear lady in the next village who'd been widowed a couple of years earlier. Locally she'd always been regarded as somewhat eccentric, but I began to realize that for 'eccentric' read 'accepting'.

Deidre asked all three of us over for Sunday lunch. We hadn't been to church. I felt too angry to worship God with all those people around who didn't want to know us any more. Instead, at Roger's instigation, we'd had a short time of prayer together. Over lunch at Deidre's that day I realized that it felt good to be together as a family. And Deidre? Her toast was 'To social pariahs, everywhere.'

I couldn't have got through the next weeks without her. She knew about social isolation, she said, because since she'd been widowed she'd realized that life revolved around couples. Deidre knew about loneliness and having to find the strength to carry on. She'd come round and spend time with Roger, quite often reading to him, because his eyesight was beginning to go. She'd help with the cleaning or the shopping, but above all she was just there—ready to listen, non-judgmental.

The only other people to stay in touch were two of Roger's friends—Sam and Timothy. They phoned almost daily, and one weekend they came to stay. I thought I'd feel uncomfortable with them, but it turned out to be a very special time. Sam told me how painful it was to attend the funeral of a partner, but be forced to creep in at the back of the chapel and hope that the family hadn't noticed. When I'd first heard stories like that, I was incredulous. Now, with our own experience, I began to realize how harsh society can be.

Another support to all of us at this time was our family doctor. He called in nearly every day, answered our questions as best he could and, if he didn't know, would go off and find out. It was he who, as Roger began to fail, found a hospice fifty miles away which would take Roger if we wanted. I wanted to keep Roger at home and let him die with us, but it was Roger himself who insisted that he should go into the hospice. He said the end would be awful, and he didn't want to think of us having to nurse him through that.

So, some four months after Roger came to live with us, he left again. This time for good. We all knew it, but we were also able to talk about it. The strength of our small family unit at that time was formidable. Thrown together, we had grown together.

Roger lived just twenty-four days and by the end I was praying that God would take him. Tony and I had moved into a hotel near the hospice so that we could spend as much time as possible with Roger. He had deteriorated rapidly. His eyesight had gone completely and he began to suffer terrible convulsions.

He was right. The end was awful. And those self-righteous people who claim that this is God's judgment on sinful people, and who treat the whole family like lepers, should spend time at the bedside of someone dying from AIDS. Is God so vengeful and morally indignant that he would send such a horrific disease as a punishment on a young man who only ever wanted to help other people, and who found that he loved another man?

No! The God I saw at work in that hospice was in the nurses who so lovingly nursed my son, with no revulsion and no prejudice; in the chaplain who spent so much time with Tony and me, encouraging us to talk about what we felt; and, of course, in dear, lovable, eccentric Deidre who was there for all of us, right the way through.

Roger's funeral was a small one, shared with the hospice staff and with Sam and Timothy as well. The service, led by the chaplain, was honest. It expressed the tragedy of a young man's life, with so much potential, so horribly extinguished; but of our relief, also, that his suffering was now over.

And the future? Tony and I returned to our family home, but together decided we couldn't bear living there. Not the house—that *felt welcoming—but the village. The place where we had been so much a part of the community had ostracized us at the very time we most needed it. I couldn't help but think how different things would have been if we'd just said that Roger had cancer. And that sickened me. No matter why someone is dying, they need support and love, as do their family.*

I look back at the time Tony and I struggled to come to terms with Roger's illness and death, and still feel very angry indeed at the way so many of our so-called friends and acquaintances rejected us. We were cast out as 'untouchables' and that hurt—deeply.

Angela's story of a taboo illness is similar to so many others—not only due to AIDS but also to suicide and to death from drug or alcohol addiction. All of these can lead to the overwhelming isolation of those left grieving, even though they may have their own conflicting feelings of anger, guilt or revulsion. At the very time they most need support, a judgmental society denies it.

Possibly it is fear that makes society behave so harshly, or a sense of moral rectitude. Yet, in the New Testament, time after time we read of how Jesus spent time with the people who were considered unclean. He knew the foibles and fallibility of human beings, but he didn't avoid them. He talked instead about a fullness of living and a better way of loving.

Steven's story

For Steven, it was not so much the disapproval of other people that was hard to take, but his own tremendous feelings of guilt. He was thirty-four when his wife, Penny, committed suicide. They had two daughters aged eleven and nine at the time.

*P*enny hadn't been herself for a couple of months. She wasn't sleeping well. I'd find her sitting downstairs, gazing into the distance. It was like she was in another world. She wasn't listening when the girls told her things that had happened at school and she stopped taking an interest in her appearance. Her hair would need washing and she stopped wearing make-up.*

I got really fed up with her behaviour. It seemed selfish and I couldn't see why she wouldn't make an effort. There were times when I tried to talk to her about what was going on, but she never said very much and I ended up getting even angrier at her. I couldn't understand what was happening and felt terribly confused. If I tried to touch Penny, just even to give her a cuddle, she recoiled.

I tried to get Penny to go and see a doctor. When she did eventually go, all he said was that she should pull herself together. Maybe if she got a job then she'd have less time to think about herself.

When I heard this I felt relieved that there was nothing wrong, but got even more irritated by Penny and the way she was making life so unpleasant for the rest of her family. She and I got to the stage where we didn't really talk any more and I noticed that the girls started to avoid her. As soon as they'd had tea they would go out to friends or up to their bedrooms. 'Mummy's no fun any more!' one of them said.

At one level I was at my wits' end. I hadn't a clue what to do for the best. And there was another bit of me that thought about walking out, leaving her to get on with it. Maybe that would shake her into action. But I couldn't do that to the girls.

Penny's parents had both died when she was sixteen, but she had a sister who I got to come and talk to Penny. She was exasperated that she couldn't seem to get through to Penny either. And when I look back I can see why we did get angry and irritated. The GP had said there was nothing wrong and so we expected Penny to 'pull herself together'.

Then Penny appeared to get a bit better. She dressed nicely, and even had lunch with a friend or two. She made more effort with the meals at home, and began smiling again. I was just relieved that, whatever the problem had been, she now seemed to be getting over it. She still wasn't sleeping very well, but it didn't seem to worry her so much.

Then one day at work I got a call from Leila, our elder daughter. Did I know where her mother was? She wasn't at home when they'd got in from school, although she had said she would be. I began to feel very uneasy. Maybe Penny had just had enough and walked out on us.

I left for home straight away. There was no note left, and none of her belongings had gone, except her handbag. I couldn't understand where she was. I phoned everyone I could think of, but no one had seen her. I talked to the neighbours, and one of them had seen her walking *down the street just after two o'clock.*

By nine I was frantic. And then the police arrived. Could they speak to my wife? When I explained the situation, they gently explained that a woman had been killed by a train early that evening. My wife's handbag had been found at the scene. They asked if my wife had been depressed recently?

I couldn't quite make sense of their words. Why was Penny on a train? Why were they asking if she'd been depressed? How had she come to lose her handbag? Gently the officer explained that the woman they thought was Penny had deliberately walked onto the track as the train was coming. No! Not possible! Penny would never do that—it can't have been her. There had to be some mistake!

It was Penny. I had to identify her by her clothes and jewellery because her body was so badly mutilated by the train. When I heard myself saying that those were Penny's things I was hit by an enormous wave of guilt. Why hadn't she said she felt so awful? Why couldn't she have told me she was thinking about suicide? If I'd known I would have been more sympathetic. I hated myself because I'd been so angry with her.

And then I thought of the GP who'd told her to go and find herself a job. If he'd stood in front of me then, I swear I would have thumped him. Why hadn't he taken her seriously? And then I thought, well I could have gone with her that time. Maybe he'd have listened to me. And why hadn't I gone? Because I'd been busy at work. If only, if only . . .

There were so many ordeals to face after Penny's suicide—trying to explain it all to the girls and then coping with the guilt and anger they felt; the inquest, where the train driver said that he'd come out of a tunnel and seen a woman, Penny, standing on the line, facing him. He'd tried to stop but there hadn't been enough time. He was terribly upset and I felt sorry for him.

I found myself uncontrollably angry with Penny that she had done this to us all. Hadn't she thought about what it was going to do to her daughters, her sister, to me, to an innocent train driver, even to the guys who'd had to pick her off the line?

The day after Penny died a letter from her arrived, addressed to me and the girls. It apologized for the pain she'd caused us, but said that we'd be better off without her. 'Don't mourn my going,' she wrote.

'I'm not worth it. But remember I love you all very much but you'll be better off without me.'

How could she ever think that? We needed her, we loved her. I was so confused. At least twenty times a day I'd think if only I'd done this, if only I'd said that. I lived in guilt and almost wouldn't have been surprised if I'd been arrested for failing to see how mentally ill my wife was. Rationally I knew it wasn't possible, but I'd almost have felt better if it had happened. I was a worthless husband, so much so I'd driven my wife to suicide.

I was like that for months. Even now, five years on, I think how different things might have been. But after a few months I thought that if I couldn't talk about how I felt, I was going to explode. At home I was trying to be strong for the girls, at work I was trying to bury myself; but inside, there was a seething mass of rage and hate and guilt.

One night I had a dream. Penny was drowning in a river and I was standing on the bank, watching her. When she called to me to help her, I shouted, 'Help yourself!' and turned my back on her and walked away. I didn't need to be Sigmund Freud to work out what that dream meant.

When I realized how much I needed to talk, my employers arranged for me to see a psychiatrist for a few sessions. She was really helpful and explained to me that, from what I'd told her of Penny and those last few months, that there was no doubt at all that she had been severely depressed. And she added that for people who are depressed and having suicidal thoughts the danger time can be when they are beginning to get back a bit more energy. Only then do they have the strength to do what they just couldn't get around to when they were at their very lowest.

In those few sessions I cried, I ranted. I still couldn't believe or accept that Penny did what she did. She had so much going for her, so much to live for. And knowing what she did about losing parents as a teenager, how could she have deliberately done it to the girls? I told all of this to the psychiatrist. She suggested that maybe I could see that it was the depression that had led Penny to commit suicide, and not Penny herself.

That's all very well, but you know, if I'd seen how mentally ill she was I'd have got her the help she needed. Instead, five years on, I can still wake up in the morning feeling guilty that I let my wife die. I might just as well have pushed her under that train for all the good I did her.

The girls? They grew up quick. They knew the truth and they seem better than me at accepting their mother was ill. Leila says to me that she knows her mother wouldn't have done it unless she'd been really, really desperate and so she doesn't blame her. Mind you, I'm not saying they didn't have problems at the time. They did. There were nightmares, tantrums, lots of sore tummies or headaches. But we pulled through together.

For a long time I thought people were avoiding me because they thought that in some way I'd been so awful to Penny that I'd driven her to it. But now I realize that they just felt awkward and didn't know what to do for the best. The best support I got was from our next-door neighbour. She would do the washing, cook us meals, help out with the shopping; and then, when we all began to pick up a bit, she showed the girls what to do if they wanted to try cooking.

Apart from the guilt which I think will be with me to the day I die, the worst thing is the loneliness. Nobody else I know who's my age has lost a wife. One or two are divorced, but that's different. I sit in, night after night, watching the girls do their homework or just watching the TV. My parents would like me to marry again, but I'm scared to get close to another woman. I feel I'm jinxed and would only bring her bad luck. I couldn't bear it if I married again and my second wife were to die.

My parents won't talk about Penny at all. Soon after she died they told me they thought there had always been something a 'bit odd' about her and that they had been disappointed when I told them we were going to get married. I was livid! This was the first I'd heard of this. I remember my mother's reaction very well. She'd been delighted, and enjoyed telling her friends 'what a nice girl' her son Steve was marrying.

We then had a huge row. They rubbished Penny, saying what a terrible wife she'd been, and how typically selfish she'd been by killing herself just because she was feeling 'a bit down'. They couldn't accept depression as a clinical condition, pooh-poohing it as psychiatrists making work for themselves.

We were all sitting around the table at the time. I asked Leila and her sister to leave the room, and then launched into a terrible tirade. I *don't want to remember some of the things I called my parents, and in the end I walked out on them and went to the pub. Sitting there, gazing at a pint, I realized how difficult they found it to say that their daughter-in-law had committed suicide. It was easier to dismiss her as 'no good' than to accept that the Penny they had really liked, had killed herself. It's not quite the thing to brag about to the neighbours!*

We made up soon after that dreadful day but we didn't talk about Penny again. I know they haven't forgiven her for what she did to me and the girls. Actually, in my heart of hearts, I'm not sure I have. Mostly it's the guilt I feel, but now and again I feel so angry at what's happened to us as a family that I frighten myself.

How can somebody like Steven ever grow beyond the confused emotions caused by the suicide of someone he loved? Many people in similar situations have turned to long-term counselling. There they can begin to understand better what is going on inside and gradually come to terms with the loss for which, to some degree, they feel responsible.

With suicide, the guilt can be more paralyzing than in any other bereavement. Somehow, though, it's essential to let it go—a seemingly simple achievement which is very difficult to achieve. Yet one life has already been cut short, is it worth ruining the remaining ones? In Steven's case he had the reassurance that his wife was mentally ill. Some people whose relatives commit suicide don't always have that reassurance. There may have been no warning signs at all. The suicide may have been prompted by circumstances that were completely unknown. Money troubles, extra-marital relationships, overwhelming stress.

There is also the tragedy of a young person who commits suicide. In America, suicide is now the third commonest death amongst young men in their teens or early twenties. Recent figures in Britain show that suicide is the third commonest cause of death in all young adults, and the trend is getting worse. It is thought that not all of these young people set out to kill themselves, but that their attempts were more cries for help. Cries of help which went desperately wrong and were heard when it was too late to do anything about them.

It is no real consolation to know that the young person

concerned may not really have meant it. The guilt is still there. 'Why didn't I notice how unhappy she was?' 'Why couldn't I tell how worried he was?' And added to that is the thought, 'If only I'd got back sooner I might have got there before it was too late.'

Suicides are such tragic deaths, full of ambivalence and the endless 'if only'. The people around may have little understanding or sympathy, and the bereaved are left—isolated by taboo and incomprehension, and racked by conflicting and confusing emotions. Is there any way through the difficult times ahead?

In the first instance it is important not to apportion blame. Although it is a normal human reaction to seek a scapegoat, it is misplaced here. We really do not need a psychological defence mechanism whereby any uneasy sense of personal responsibility can be laid at someone else's feet. In the aftermath of a suicide, anger could be directed towards almost everyone: police, doctors, other family members, self, and the person who has died. But if we start blaming, the internal spiral of guilt and resentment begins to destroy the very relationships which should sustain us at this horrendous time.

Steven's relationship with his parents almost foundered when there had already been the catastrophic self-destruction of suicide. It is crucial instead to try and maintain relationships in which support and sharing the pain can take place.

Although suicide has not been a crime for a long time, there is still a stigma attached to it. There is acute sensitivity to the looks and thoughts of people outside the family, fear of judgment and blame. Sadly, the reactions of outsiders can cause even more anger and guilt. 'Let them mind their own business,' we snap. And then we think, 'Maybe they've got a point.' We need to face these contradictory feelings and work through the pain and horror, confronting them rather than ignoring them. Only then will they ease.

The first step to coming to terms with our feelings is to find a good listener. It may be a professional counsellor (or a health visitor, a doctor or a minister). It could be a good friend although they, in turn, may need support. Whoever we turn to, we need to talk it all out, if necessary going over the same ground again and again. We need someone who won't judge, who won't try to deny our feelings and who will listen not just once but many times.

Some people bereaved by suicide encounter the supposedly well-meaning friend, who says, 'Well, as they meant to kill themselves, there's no need to grieve. They wanted to die!' This is the classic attitude of those who want to distance themselves from pain. They feel better by saying it, but the recipient doesn't. It completely denies the feelings of all who are left grieving, just like the person who crosses the road to avoid having to talk to bereaved people. The key thing to remember is, 'Even if the person I loved wanted to die, I didn't want them to die. That's why I have every right to mourn.'

For Christians it may be particularly hard to accept suicide. Life is a gift given by God and it ends in its due course. Biblical teaching holds that life is sacred and not to be ended by human hands. So there may be enormous concern and fear that someone who has committed suicide is now in outer darkness or some other banishment from God's love. The church itself used to insist that those who died by suicide had to be buried in unconsecrated ground.

However, what we really need to fix our eyes upon as Christians is neither the church nor social attitudes, but God. For in God we see that love is the prime mover, and when he knows and shares our pain we paradoxically receive his healing. If, in the deepest depression and mental illness, in great anxiety or overwhelming stress, someone has found it impossible to go on, is that person so much more sinful than any other? Of course not; and God in his infinite mercy knows that far more than we ever can.

TABOO DEATHS

☐ 'Taboo deaths' are the result of the more complicated, less comfortable sides of human nature. Disturbing inner turmoil, different ways of expressing sexuality, or thoughts of self-destruction are often things which we try to ignore. They are unnerving.

☐ The strength of feeling which leads to willful self-destruction seems to stray beyond society's norm. Those bereaved as a result can find themselves socially isolated. The pain they suffer is an unwelcome reminder to others of the unknown depth of human complexity. Society and the people who make up society do not like to confront the shadow side of life. After all, isn't it much easier to condemn than it is to try to understand?

9

EVERYONE CAN FEEL LOSS

*All my life I've felt that my mother didn't really die. I'm
seventy now, and my mother died when I was six. I didn't
go to her funeral, and nobody ever really talked about her
again. I used to think that she'd run away. Even now,
when I've seen her grave, it doesn't seem very real.*

---

*I couldn't bring myself to tell our four year old, Helen,
that her baby sister had died in hospital. We didn't think
she was old enough to understand and just said Sophie
had gone away. But we had a terrible time with Helen.
Her behaviour was dreadful, she wouldn't settle at night
and she started to wet the bed again. The health visitor
said Helen was grieving for her sister.*

---

*People think my son Paul is 'not with it'. He was brain-
damaged when he was born. He's now twenty and goes to
a day centre for people with learning difficulties. But when
his father died, Paul sensed how sad I was and came and
held me. I told him his dad had died and he came with me
to see him at the rest-home. Paul cried and knew only too
well what the death of his father meant.*

How much children should be told about death seems to vary
from one extreme to another. There are parents who feel that

their children should be protected at all costs from any notion of death or dying; and there are those who believe that from a very early age children are able to feel loss. And if they are able to feel loss then the cause of that loss needs to be honestly, but gently, explained.

Loss is also felt by children and adults who have learning difficulties (what used to be known as 'mental handicap'). It can be felt, too, by much older adults whose mental processes may have been affected—for instance by senile dementia, or Alzheimer's disease. Just because a person seems inarticulate or confused, it doesn't mean that they cannot feel loss and be affected by it. Wherever there has been a relationship, even if the bereaved person doesn't seem to be what we might unfeelingly call 'normal', then an end to that relationship will be felt. As long as we are conscious we will feel loss, no matter how altered our consiousness becomes.

The first time I encountered people with learning difficulties I was terrified. The visit was part of a sixth-form community involvement programme and the aim was to widen our experience of life outside school. It certainly did that and over the weeks we visited, my terror left. I soon realized the enormous capacity for love and affection shown by people who were born with learning difficulties or who later develop them. This love and affection isn't always expressed in the usual way, it's often more poignant and meaningful than that.

Some years on from that experience at school, I was involved in making several television programmes with the l'Arche communities. Through the various encounters, and particularly through the deep spirituality there, I have come to realize how wrong it is to dismiss people with learning difficulties as if they were subhuman. Their feelings and emotions and their capacity to love are just as great as anyone else's. And that means they feel loss to an equal extent.

This chapter therefore discusses how best to deal with bereavement in children, or in people who have learning difficulties, or in those who are elderly and confused.

CHILDREN

Children pick up so much from the attitudes and behaviour of the people around them. If they are excluded in a bereavement on the grounds that it is too distressing for them to be told the truth, they will still pick up on the distress of the adults. Puzzled by what is going on around them and feeling that it must be something awful if they are not allowed to be part of it, they begin to form an attitude towards death which they may take with them right into adulthood.

This attitude may be that death is a taboo subject and not to be talked about as part of everyday conversation. Sadly, it will also mean that the child is poorly prepared for grief in adulthood.

The same attitude may also incorporate some unnecessary guilt. Young children see themselves as being at the centre of their world, and in the event of a death close to them it is common for them to believe they are at fault. Many even think that they have somehow killed off the person they love (or hate) and that they have caused the whole sequence of events. One child in a foster home not so long ago was heard to say in his goodnight prayers, 'Dear God, please tell Mummy that when I killed her it wasn't my fault.' The mother of the child in question had died in a car crash, and the child had been nowhere near the scene at all.

How do we prevent such ideas forming? How on earth does one begin to explain to a child what death is? If the child has lost a parent or someone else close to them, how can they be helped through the grief they will be feeling? These are hard issues to address, especially if the person closest to the bereaved child is suffering the same loss and is not therefore in the best of states to handle the feelings of anyone else.

If at all possible, the key is to acknowledge the shared loss and grieve together. We must mourn together where possible, and deal honestly and gently with the child concerned.

Shirley's story

Shirley's husband, Roy, was diagnosed as having liver cancer when their two children were aged nine and four. Tests had shown that Roy's cancer was beyond treatment and nothing could be done except to relieve the pain. The doctors thought that he only had a very short time left to live.

Roy came home from the hospital as both Shirley and he wanted him to be at home when he died. Their children, Alice and Daniel, only knew that their father wasn't well and, although both parents wanted them to know about the cancer, the question was how to tell them.

F or the first few days Roy was at home we said nothing to the kids. They just knew that 'Daddy was still feeling poorly'. But other family members knew and, of course, came to visit. Roy's parents were still alive and deeply upset by the news, as were close friends. When Roy had gone into hospital, he'd never dreamt for a moment that he was so seriously ill. But it had got to the point where something had to be said to the children because sooner or later they were likely to hear something or sense that all was not right.

The amazing thing was, before we'd decided what to say, Alice, our older one, just came straight out with it.

It was one afternoon when she was sitting on Roy's knee watching TV. I was out shopping at the time with Dan. Apparently she'd asked her Dad how poorly he really was, and when Roy said why was she asking she said it was because everyone who came to the house was now sad. And that they were being really nice to her and Daniel, which she said was kind of weird!

She's very observant, Alice, and she was probably picking up on all our apprehension. When he said, well, he was quite poorly, she quite simply asked him if he was going to die.

I think up till then Roy had found it hard enough to admit it to himself, let alone our nine-year-old daughter. But he just said yes, that he was going to die. And soon. He said that of course he didn't want to leave us all, but that he had cancer and that the doctors couldn't make him better. He was very good with her, very honest. He said he was going to get more and more sick and not able to do things he liked any more. And Alice just took it, and understood.

When Dan and I got back we found them in tears, cuddling one another. I knew at once what had happened, so then I told Dan. It was hard, and all I could say was, 'Dan, we're all crying because Daddy is very, very sick. He's not going to get better. He's going to die soon.'

Dan just looked bemused and puzzled, so I picked him up and we joined Roy and Alice on the settee. Dan asked if he could go with Roy when he died, he was so sweet and concerned. And Roy just said, 'Dan, that's a really nice thought. It would be good to have company, but I've got to die on my own. You've got lots of years in front of you to live here with Mummy and Alice.'

And then came the question, 'But what do you do when you're dead?' I groaned inwardly—honestly, the capacity of children to ask the questions everyone would love to know the answers to! But Roy was wonderful, and he said, 'I don't know what I'll do when I'm dead, Dan; that's the mystery. But I'll find out soon. I'm not frightened by it, though. And I'm sure I'm going to heaven and that I'll meet my granny and grandad there, and I hope I'll see Jesus, too.'

It's odd, but though it was agonizing telling the children that Roy was dying, we also felt huge relief. Everything was out in the open and the children were free to ask or say whatever they wanted to.

We almost enjoyed the next few days together. Dan and Alice spent a lot of time with Roy, playing games, reading, or just laying on the bed with him, watching TV. But it was soon obvious that Roy was deteriorating. The doctor increased his pain medication and district nurses began visiting more. And Roy began to spend more and more time sleeping.

I was really worried about what to do with Dan and Alice. I wondered if they could go and stay with my mum to spare them the pain of watching Roy die. But I wasn't sure. Eventually a good friend of mine, Mandy, offered to come and live with us. She had always got on well with the children and it seemed to be the best solution all round. I could spend time with Roy without worrying about Alice and Dan, and looking after them. And the kids were able to be with their father if they wanted to.

One sad thing was to see Roy's parents age so much—almost overnight. They came as often as they could, but they'd taken a terrible blow. And it was only about a week after Mandy moved in that the doctor said she didn't think Roy would be conscious much longer.

I remember Dan was playing on the floor of his father's room, and very soon Alice came racing in from school, making a beeline for Roy. This had become the pattern ever since they had known how ill he was. Roy enjoyed it, and the children had chosen it.

I just about managed to talk to both of them over tea that day. I explained that the doctor had said that Daddy was going to die very soon now, and that what would happen next would be that he would go into a deep sleep. He wouldn't wake up again, and that maybe tonight when they kissed Daddy goodnight they might like to make it a special kiss.

Roy knew it wouldn't be long, too, and he wanted his painkilling injections to be delayed for a bit so that he was more alert for the time he could spend with Dan and Alice. It was an incredibly special time for us all. Roy gave each of the kids a photograph album which he'd put together so that when they were older they had something to remember their dad by.

Then by the time Roy's parents arrived, Dan was already in bed. Alice asked if she could stay up and of course I said yes. Roy was sort of drifting in and out of sleep. I'd try and reassure him, saying everything was fine, and that we loved him.

By midnight Alice was hardly to keep her eyes open, bless her. So she gave Roy a kiss, and I put her to bed. And then there were just the three of us—Roy's parents and me—watching and waiting. During the night, his breathing became more and more laboured and by dawn I really began to think that each breath just had to be the last. I said things quietly, saying it was all right and that he could go now. But inside I felt panic. How on earth would we cope on our own? And at the same time, I felt as if I was in a dream, and that soon I'd wake up and everything would be back to normal. I couldn't quite believe that Roy really was dying.

But he did die. He died at 6.30 that morning. His parents moved into the lounge to leave me on my own. Dan was first up and he popped his head round the door; and he knew without me saying anything. Without saying a word he just hugged me and looked at his dad and kissed him.

Then Alice came, and do you know what she said? She was upset, it's true, but all she said was, 'Daddy will be happy now. He'd been so poorly and he won't be hurting now, will he?' And then she sat by him, crying softly. She didn't stay long and when we left and joined the others in the kitchen she said, 'That didn't really look like Daddy. He looked different!'

I felt relieved that Alice and Dan were there to share this with me.

I was very shaken, and although I'd had time to prepare for Roy's death, nothing really prepares you for the awful finality of it. Maybe it was selfish to have the children there, but I felt that it was also right that they should have had the chance to say goodbye.

The next hurdle was the funeral. I wasn't at all sure how I was going to get through it on my own, let alone with the children. But they had been so much part of all that we'd been through that I asked if they wanted to come. Of course they wanted to come! Mandy was there as well, and beforehand we explained what would happen and tried to prepare them as much as we could. I didn't want it to be too distressing for them.

All that was two years ago now. There have been moments when one of the children wants to know why Roy died, and I have to say to them, 'I just don't know!' I didn't want to say things to them like, 'Well, God wanted Daddy to go and live with him now,' because I can't accept that, so I don't see why they should. They go to church and to Sunday school and they say their prayers every night, but I feel it's wrong for them to think of God as deliberately taking their daddy from them.

I'm glad that they remained in the house, though, and didn't go to my mother's, because in the same way that I've lost my husband they've lost their father. It meant such a lot to Roy to have them there, and when he knew they were due back from school he always made an effort to look presentable. I think being there helped the children understand all that happened. They saw how sick their father was, and I think they saw that death needn't be frightening.

They still talk about Roy a lot. Sometimes it's just wishing he was about and when Father's Day comes round in June, we go and visit Roy's grave and put fresh flowers there. It's hard on them because at school all the kids are talking about Father's Day, and my two are reminded that they no longer have a father. Obviously there are children in their school whose parents are divorced but most of them still see their fathers. So if the younger ones make cards for their dads, Dan makes his for his grandad.

I went to see Dan and Alice's teachers when Roy was first diagnosed, and made sure they knew, too, when Roy had died. The teachers seemed grateful I'd done that, and certainly Alice's teacher talked to the whole class about what had happened when Alice was off *for those few days around the funeral. I also made sure that the teachers knew what we'd told the children and asked them to say the same thing if Dan or Alice asked them. I didn't want them to be given different versions of what death is. We'd tried to be as honest as we could, and if we didn't know, we said so. And that's been my attitude right through these last two years. If I'm feeling particularly down and they notice, then I'll say that I'm missing their daddy; and if they want answers to questions that are unanswerable even by adults, then I'll say I don't know. I've come to realize more and more that if you're honest with children, accepting the limits to their comprehension, then that's the best thing to do. It's tough, but sometimes it's a tough world.*

I've told the story of Shirley and Roy at some length because it shows how a family can tackle the issue of bereavement in children. It also shows what a very great deal of strength the children gave the adults. Think what the alternative might have been: sent away to their Granny's, occasionally visiting Daddy at home, and then being sent away again—finally to be told, 'Daddy has gone away'.

It is worth remembering that children can get stuck in their grief in the same way that adults can, if the experience is really handled badly. Emotional development and educational progress can suddenly cease or go backwards, and even mechanical skills of co-ordination or managing daily routines can be affected. Years later, the suppressed grief will eventually show in quite different forms, such as delaying tactics, phobias, playing life's 'victim', or deeply rebellious behaviour.

Fortunately the death of a parent is comparatively rare. But children will still encounter death. Their grandparents may die, or other adults such as teachers or neighbours. It may even be the death of a school friend. Shirley's account of how she tried to be open and honest with her children is applicable in these circumstances too.

Also, how many pets, from hamsters through to cats and dogs, do children lose in the course of their childhood? All of these are occasions when children can begin to understand what death is. Simple funeral services for animals with a burial in the garden or common ground, conducted by the children themselves, can be both poignant and comical. Yet they are an opportunity to grieve and to begin to accept the loss of a much loved companion.

Death cannot be hidden from children. They see it on the TV and it's the stuff of their play, 'Bang! Bang! You're dead!' Use the opportunities as they occur to talk openly and honestly about death.

LEARNING DIFFICULTIES

Twenty years ago, Kate and Robert had thought that they would never be able to have a child of their own. Then, when Kate was almost forty, she discovered that she was pregnant. Delighted, she and Robert planned for the arrival of their much wanted baby.

When Polly was born, however, the hospital staff were subdued. A consultant was called for and Polly was hurried away. Neither Kate nor Robert were able to hold her and they were told their baby daughter was very ill.

Polly pulled through, as Kate and Robert kept an anxious vigil by her cot. One day they were called in to talk with the consultant. Gently they were told that Polly may have suffered brain damage and that she also had Down's Syndrome. They were told that Polly had little chance of a normal life.

N *ormal! Normal! What's normal? People are so ready to write off those they consider to be different. Polly was our daughter and Robert and I intended to look after her, no matter how disabled she was.*

Polly came home to live with us. She was a beautiful child, happy, full of fun and affectionate. Even now, so many years later, she never says more than a few words, but she doesn't have to be able to say, 'I love you'. When she throws her arms around me, and gives me a great big kiss, I know she loves me—and I love her, too.

But then last year, when Polly was nineteen, Robert died. He was on his motor bike, on his way home, when a car hit him. The driver never stopped. Robert was taken to hospital, unconscious and critically ill. He never regained consciousness and died two days later.

When I first heard of Robert's accident, Polly was out at a club she attended. I asked a good friend, Phil, to meet her and take her back to his family. 'Tell Polly I've gone shopping,' I said. Then I raced to the hospital and discovered how critically ill Robert was. I was absolutely distraught and time just stopped as I sat there, willing him to live.

I've no idea how much later it was, but a nurse came to me, saying that somebody called Phil insisted that he had to talk to me. Phil?

Polly! How could I forget her! Phil told me that she wouldn't settle. She was huddled in the corner of the room, banging her head on the wall. He said Polly was really disturbed, and he just didn't know what to do for the best—bring her to the hospital or ask a doctor to call.

My instinct was that he should bring her to the hospital. Robert was so ill, and maybe seeing him would help Polly. We'd never talked to her about death, and I wasn't at all sure how she would respond now. But somehow Phil had to warn her. It wouldn't be fair for her to see him without knowing he was sick. I told Phil to tell Polly that her dad was very sick and to clutch his stomach. She would understand that.

Seemingly, as soon as he did that, Polly began to calm down. In no time at all, they were at the hospital and we met up at the Intensive Care Unit. Polly rushed to hug me, and cried. An understanding nurse took one of Polly's hands and I held the other, and we walked with her into the room where Robert was. She stood still, looking intently at the bed. For a second I thought I'd made a mistake, but then she moved forward and gently touched Robert's hand. She looked puzzled that he didn't respond, and touched him again, harder this time.

I began to cry then, uncontrollably. I couldn't be strong any longer. As the nurse tried to comfort me, a huge bear-hug grabbed me. Polly's hugs are unique, and I knew immediately who it was. We cried together. She understood how sick Robert was.

The day Robert died, I was on my own with him and had time to say my own goodbyes. Polly was back with Phil and his family, although she'd been at the hospital several times. Each time she'd been very quiet, and studied Robert closely. Now she came back to see him in death.

He looked at rest. A bandage covered his battered head, but the tubes and machines of intensive care had gone. Polly came in, looked, touched, and I told her Robert had died. There was no way I could explain to her what that meant, but she touched Robert again, and then slowly began to stroke his face. Her voice made the noises which she makes when she's unhappy. On and on they went, and I could do nothing to ease her pain. I cried again. 'It's just you and me now, Polly,' I said as we left the hospital together.

That night she slept in the bed beside me. She slept heavily and I dozed, thankful for her warmth beside me yet at the same time longing for that warmth to be Robert. Next morning, as people began to call round at the house, Polly wouldn't leave my side. She held my hand until it hurt, and with her other she clutched one of Robert's jumpers. She knew that Robert had gone, and was scared that I might go to.

Over the next few weeks Polly sensed my own pain, too. She was very gentle and stroked me a lot. When she found me in tears she would rock me from side to side, as a mother does with a baby. At Robert's funeral, which I very much wanted her to be a part of, Polly helped the vicar light four candles around the coffin. He told the congregation that they were for Robert, Polly's dad, and Polly nodded wisely. At the end of the service, after the coffin had disappeared behind the curtains of the crematorium, Polly blew the candles out.

As I lived with my grief, and struggled to survive without Robert, I know that Polly grieved too. She hadn't the words to say what she was feeling, but I knew she missed her dad. To this day I'm glad that Phil phoned the hospital, and risked disturbing me at a private time. Afterwards he told me how he very nearly hadn't, but he just felt sure, seeing how disturbed Polly was, that, somehow, she knew something terrible had happened. She needed to see Robert, in the same way that any other child would want to see her dad. I'm glad she came, that I didn't exclude her in the mistaken belief that she wouldn't understand, and that we were able to share the grief we both felt with Robert's death.

OLD AGE

Although this next account relates to the particular circumstance of old age, it could well have happened to a younger person suffering from Alzheimer's disease (pre-senile dementia), or from any mental condition which produces confusion, loss of memory or unpredictable behaviour. The fundamental fact is that even if we think there is no hope of understanding that a loved one has died, we can never be certain. Indeed, most of the evidence goes to show that we would be wrong.

Peggy and Arnold's story

Every day since Peggy had gone into a nursing home after a bad stroke, her husband Arnold walked up the hill to visit her. They had been married for sixty years, and he was devoted to her. He didn't always stay long, but he would sit beside Peggy, holding her hand and talking to her about whatever he could. Peggy's stroke had deprived her of speech and she seemed to have difficulty understanding what was said to her. Her left side was paralyzed, and she was confined to bed.

Sometimes she'd get confused and upset, and the nursing staff wondered if Peggy really knew where she was. But when Arnold sat beside her, her eyes met his and she knew exactly who he was.

Then, one day, Arnold didn't come to the nursing home. Nobody had heard from him and the staff were concerned. The local church minister takes up the story:

I'd come to know Arnold and Peggy well. I had enormous admiration for the way that Arnold went to visit Peggy day in day out. A couple of times I was with Peggy when he arrived, and her eyes would just light up when she saw him.

When I heard that he hadn't visited that day I was concerned and went round to his home. The milk was on the doorstep, the curtains were drawn. There was no reply when I shouted through the letterbox, so I called the police.

Arnold was dead. He was in bed, in his pyjamas, as if he'd died peacefully in his sleep. For Arnold there were going to be no more daily walks up that steep hill to the nursing home. But Peggy? Would she understand that Arnold had died? She was terribly confused and it was only when she saw Arnold that something seemed to register.

Heading back to the nursing home I wondered how best to tell Peggy. Maybe I shouldn't try and tell her? Would she notice that Arnold wasn't visiting any more? But she deserved to be treated with dignity and respect. Who was I to judge what Peggy may or may not understand? *Her husband had died and I would try and tell her.*

As I walked up to Peggy's bed, her eyes opened and then closed as soon as she saw it was me. Although I had sat with Peggy many times now, she never recognized me when I came back. Arnold, and Arnold alone, she seemed to know.

I called Peggy's name several times and eventually she opened her eyes, looking blankly at me. I introduced myself again, took her hand, and then asked, 'Are you waiting for Arnold, Peggy?' This time there was a flicker of interest. So, as gently as I could, I told Peggy that Arnold had died.

She looked right through me. I tried again, this time taking the photo of Arnold which sat on her locker. One solitary tear formed and ran slowly down her cheek. Her good hand tightened round mine and I knew that Peggy understood. I said a prayer, and as I did so, her grip on me slackened. Peggy had gone to sleep.

Within twenty-four hours, Peggy herself had died. It was as if Arnold had been her reason for hanging on to life. Knowing that he was gone, she gave up the fight.

We know so little about the way the human brain functions. Someone may appear to have no recognition, or to live in a confused state, but we cannot be certain how much information they are able to take in. In the event of the death of someone close to them, it is important to find ways of telling them and helping them to grieve.

If a person is too ill to attend a funeral service, a hospital chaplain can hold a service at the bedside at the same time as the funeral is happening at the grave side or the crematorium. In this way, the ill person is not excluded, and the service may be an important part of recognizing the reality of the death.

EVERYONE CAN FEEL LOSS

☐ Although all of the accounts in this chapter relate to circumstances that are relatively rare, there are truths there for all of us.

☐ We all feel loss—adults, children, people with learning difficulties, the confused elderly. No one is an exception. We might try to protect ourselves or others from the pain of that loss, but grief will be there. It is the price we pay for loving. We may try and hide from the grief or suppress it, but sooner or later it will emerge.

☐ We have no right to assume that others will not feel their loss, or understand it. Although we may want to protect them from pain, to spare their suffering, human beings glean information in more ways than words. The desire to protect may result in confusion and anxiety, as the person we're trying to protect senses that something is wrong.

☐ Everyone has the right to know the truth. And truth needs to be told—with sensitivity, compassion and, above all, love.

10

PUTTING THE PIECES BACK TOGETHER AGAIN

The thing which helps me most is meeting with other parents who also lost a child. I know it sounds morbid, but it isn't. We meet every month and there are only a few of us, so people feel free to talk, or to cry. Having the chance to say how things have gone means so much to me.

———

Soon after Joe, my husband, died, I asked my daughter to clear out all his belongings. I couldn't bear to see them around the house. Now I wish I hadn't done that; I have so little to remind me of him. Fortunately my daughter kept some of his drawings and books because she thought there might be a time when I'd appreciate them. At least I've got those.

———

My night-time strategy was this. I bought a portable TV for the bedroom, and then every night I went to bed armed with a good book, a flask of decaffeinated coffee and something to nibble, say a biscuit or an apple. Sometimes I didn't need them, but more often than not I'd wake in the night. Then, when I felt ready, I normally slept again.

———

It's been said before in this book but it's important to repeat it here: grief needs to be faced and lived through. It might seem a useful strategy to try to find ways of numbing or denying the pain we feel, but the feelings are there and the danger is that we just force them underground.

There are, however, ways in which we can make it easier for ourselves to live through the pain. Much of what follows in this chapter is based on the experience of people who have found things which worked for them or, indeed, which didn't work.

NUMBING THE PAIN

Tranquillizers, sleeping pills and antidepressants are all commonly prescribed drugs for people who are newly bereaved. Another common drug which people use is alcohol. The trouble with all of them is that they can only be used to mask the pain. It might seem as if they are 'making the pain go away' but the effect is only temporary and 'anaesthetic'. When the effect wears off, the pain comes back.

While it's true that a temporary break may be helpful, the problem comes when 'temporary' turns to permanent. A glass or two of a favourite tipple can be a useful way to help someone relax, unless the doctor has prescribed medication which clearly precludes it. But regular, heavy drinking, or deliberately setting out to drink in order to forget the grief, is dangerous—the person concerned needs to talk to someone about their grief and all that they are feeling or, perhaps, trying not to feel.

Similarly, a sleeping pill to help break a pattern of insomnia is not going to harm anyone and may be of great help. But the use of them night after night can lead to a dependent pattern and sleep becomes impossible without the pills. Also, as anyone who has done it will testify, stopping a habit of tranquillizers is extremely painful in itself.

Tranquillizers and antidepressants are different. Tranquillizers have an almost immediate effect whereas antidepressants build up in the body over a period of about two weeks, after which they begin to work. In cases of genuine clinical depression antidepressants have a useful role to play, but sadness after a death is not necessarily a clinical depression. Mourning is a normal human response to loss. To mourn is not to be depressed, but prolonged mourning can lead to, or be a sign of, depression.

Many people blithely talk about feeling depressed, but what they probably mean is they're a bit fed up. The illness of depression is much more than that. If a doctor diagnoses clinical depression and prescribes antidepressants then the body needs them and no one should worry about taking them.

Tranquillizers, on the other hand, may well be prescribed for the newly bereaved because they work quickly and there may indeed be times when their short-term use is appropriate. In the longer term, however, as has already been pointed out, tranquillizers are addictive. What really adds insult to injury is that they also store up trouble for the future by blocking the grief within.

Geraldine's story

M y husband's death came like a bolt from the blue when I was fifty-one years old. It was a tremendous shock. My GP prescribed some tranquillizers and I felt they helped. So I asked for some more, and when they came to an end I tried coping without them. But I felt so awful that I asked if I could go back on them again. My GP said nothing about addiction and happily wrote out another prescription.

It was about five years later that I was forced to face the issue when I saw a television programme about addiction, and a woman described how she'd been trying to stop taking tranquillizers and what a dreadful struggle that had been. 'I haven't got a problem,' I reassured myself, and decided to prove it.

It was awful! Panic attacks, agoraphobia, insomnia, shaking, sweating, fearful anxiety. I became a complete mess. Only the support of friends, family, and the professional help of a psychiatrist saw me through. Now I realize that, while I thought I was successfully blocking the pain that Frank's death caused me, I was hiding from it. So not only did I have to face some of that still, I also had to cope with the withdrawal symptoms.

My advice to anyone who finds themself using tranquillizers to anaesthetize their grief is to come off them under medical supervision. Hopefully they will not be addicted, and life is eventually better *without them. When I look back I might just as well have been a robot for the five years I took them.*

MOVING HOUSE

One of the biggest decisions to be faced by new widows or widowers is what to do with their home. Some want above all to stay in the place they feel closest to the person who died. Others want the complete opposite: the home becomes too painful a reminder of the past and they want to rid themselves of it as soon as possible.

Sometimes there is no choice in the matter. A move is forced because finance dictates—death duty, legal disputes, bills—so that in addition to the loss of a partner, there is also loss of all the security that home represented.

Even if there is a choice, there are probably good practical reasons to move. Financially it can make sense to move to somewhere smaller, and it may make it easier having a smaller home to look after. The key point, however, is to take time before coming to any decision. The first year after the death of a partner is an emotional roller-coaster. What someone feels at three months is not necessarily what they will feel a year later. Unless there are pressing reasons to move, it is better to stay put until a long-term decision can be made—one based on what is right for the future, not on what feels good in the heat of the moment.

Ruth's story

Ruth was sixty-three when her husband, Laurie, died at home after a three-year illness. They had been married for forty years and had two daughters who had both long since moved away into their own homes. Ruth stayed for eighteen months in the home she and Laurie had lived in for the last thirty-five years, but then she put the house on the market and was able to buy somewhere smaller in the same village.

I would have been crazy to move anywhere else. I've some really good friends here, and it's a place I love and feel safe in. But the family home was just too big for me. To be truthful it had been too big

140

for just Laurie and me after the girls left home, but it was a lovely house and neither of us really wanted to move. But when Laurie died I had to look to the future. There's going to come a time when I'm not as strong as I am now and I need somewhere I can look after easily.

For the first eighteen months after Laurie's death I needed to be in the house. It held so many memories. Straight after his death I went to stay with one of my daughters but I think that was a mistake. Everything was unfamiliar. Don't get me wrong, it was nice to be cosseted and cared for, but it was a different bed, a different house, and her daily life was different. I felt a bit in the way. So when I did go back to my own home, although I was dreading being on my own there, it was where I needed to be. It was so reassuring to hear the old central heating system clanking along through the evening, and to have all sorts of things which reminded me of Laurie around the place: his clothes, his books, his treasured pipes.

When I decided to move, I was amazed at the girls' reaction. They hadn't lived there for at least eight years, but neither of them wanted me to sell. They kept telling me I'd regret it and it was too soon. But I knew the time was right. My life now was as a single person, and that house was too big. Also, I'd said my goodbyes to Laurie. I still missed him, but it was time for me to move on.

Eventually I was able to have a long discussion with my daughters. Their advice not to sell had more to do with the fact that they didn't want me to sell! Neither of them had completed their own grieving for their father. As long as the family house remained, they could almost kid themselves that life hadn't really changed when their father died. That weekend, when they helped me move, they realized what they had been doing, and although we cried a lot for a few days, it was good. We had dinner on the last night, perched on packing cases—Chinese take-away and champagne! I raised my glass and toasted Laurie. Something like, 'Laurie, wherever you are, thank you. You were a great husband, a loving dad, and this house meant so much. Be at rest!'

Well, I've always been one for the dramatics, but it marked the end of an era, and it seemed right to do it. The next day, I moved. Sometimes I think Laurie would have hated this cottage but I have to remind myself that this is my home. Everything's very feminine, particularly my bedroom! It's manageable, it's pretty, and it's home!

Ruth is keen to live independently as long as she can. Many people at her age would probably want to do something similar. But she remembers a widower in the village, a bit older than herself, who moved in with his son and daughter-in-law for good.

It was tragic. He aged so quickly and seemed to lose his confidence. People said that he never recovered from losing his wife. I'm sure that to some extent that's because he lost parts of himself when he moved in with his son. They only live five miles away but he gave up coming over here to play bowls. And he used to be so involved in the local church, but soon gave that up as well. He became very dependent on his son, and although it all happened for the best of motives, I can't but help think it was the wrong thing to do. He seemed to lose all interest in living and it was only nine months later that he died in his sleep one night.

Home is such an important and basic part of life that it is worth being absolutely sure that the decision is the right one. The only way to be sure of this is not to rush into any decision one way or the other, until it's clear what is best. If someone is rushing to make changes about where they live, they need just to pause to ask what the rush is. Undue haste may mean not thinking through all the implications, and feelings of grief can cloud decision making. It really is better to have as little change as possible for the first year.

After all, ahead of us is the rest of our life, however long or short that may be. Bereavement is one of the greatest stresses a human being ever has to face. It's important to give the future a good start and a lot of that future will be influenced by the choice of where to live.

If after a year or so someone is still undecided about what to do, they could usefully think about what they would like to do in the future. How old are they? What is their health like? Is the home they live in at the moment too big to cope with, if not now, say in five years' time? Where do most of their friends live? Where are the activities they take part in now, or might do in the future? How would they feel about leaving their current home? What are the advantages if they stay? How do they feel about moving?

Of course, it may be that a person finally decides the best plan would be to continue where they are. If so, then fine. They need to stay put and ignore any well-meant advice trying to persuade them to move!

But what of the people who are forced to move after a death, sometimes almost immediately? Perhaps they have tied accommodation, or are suffering financial hardship. Here there is no opportunity to take time to think what to do for the best, no choice to move or not to move.

In such cases, it may be possible to 'buy time' to allow the emotional turmoil to ease, after which a more permanent decision can be taken.

Elsie's story

Elsie had lived all her adult life in homes which were tied to her husband's work. When Ken died she had three months to move out.

A t first I panicked. I didn't know where to start. Ken and I had never discussed what I'd do if he died first and I'd always avoided thinking about it. We had no children, and although his pension would give me a bit of financial security, it certainly wasn't going to run to a mortgage.

A friend, Belinda, stepped in to help. She took me down to the city housing department where they said they would try and help. But the waiting lists were long, even for people like me who were homeless. Homeless! I hated the phrase. That night I sat up all night long, terrified about the future, and longing so much for Ken that I even thought about killing myself to be with him.

With Belinda's help I began to devise a plan for the future. She warned me about making rash decisions out of panic, and helped me find thinking and recovering time. We worked out that if I stayed in the area, some things at least were familiar—shops, the church, and particularly, friends.

Belinda helped me find a rented flat near her. She'd offered me a room in her house, but I wanted to be on my own. The sooner I learned

*to stand on my own two feet, the better! It was a tiny flat, not very
attractive, and a lot of the furniture Ken and I had bought had to be
sold. But my favourite things, the ones which held good memories of
our life together, went into storage until I could sort out a more
permanent option.*

*I stayed in that tiny flat for almost a year, but in the meantime
found a housing association with property I could move into. It felt
good to plan where I would put the furniture which was in storage.
And I reached a stage where I was looking forward to moving again.
This would be my permanent home, and that felt good!*

Elsie was able to keep some of her options open until she knew,
in her own time, what she most wanted to do. If a quick move is
forced for any reason, it is important to try to find temporary
solutions. Staying with friends, family, or maybe even finding
rented property like Elsie did, can help. It's all about finding
somewhere to stay, which isn't binding but which buys time.

It is, however, good to keep some things familiar. Bereavement
is such a gigantic change that we need some stability. People we
know and who know us are vital. Where are the places and who
are the people from whom we can draw comfort and support?
What are the things in our homes which remind us now, and will
remind us in the future, of the person we have lost? We need to
keep them safe. At present they may only be a sad reminder of all
that is lost but in time we will treasure them for the good
memories they hold.

REBUILDING A LIFE

How much this section is relevant will depend on the nature of
the bereavement. Much of what follows is related to surviving
after the loss of a spouse, but there are elements which, with a
bit of adaptation, are appropriate for most major bereavements.

The key to rebuilding a life after losing someone close is to
realize that no one will never get back to life as it was before.
There has been an irrevocable change, and the journey through
grief engendered by that loss will be about adapting to the
change, not about trying to pretend it hasn't happened.

If those who are now on their own were involved in nursing the person who died, it may be that time now weighs heavily on their hands. No doubt before the death there was always something that needed to be done (the washing, changing the bedlinen, cooking) and they may have had people popping in and out of the house all day. Not just friends and family, but district nurses, GPs, ministers. And now, it's all gone quiet and they can't think what to do next.

Even if there was no home care involved, it may be that the time before the death became a very intense time. The normal daily routines may have been overtaken by what some have described as living at the very heart of life itself. Acutely aware of the proximity of death, everyday concerns would have been forgotten in the face of the big issues of life and death.

But then came the death. There would have been a lot of activity, things to be done, arrangements to be made. And now? Nothing! All that's left is the future, alone. And that can look very scary indeed, especially if there has been a sense of living in that twilight existence created by coming close to the other world, the world of heaven and eternity. Everyday matters still seem like irrelevances. Yet, in the weeks and months ahead, the grieving person needs gradually to get used to normality in this world again.

Vivienne's story

Vivienne and her family were devastated by a death at the beginning of the summer holidays. She was forty-four when her husband died suddenly. She was left with a son of sixteen and a daughter of eighteen. In September Gemma, the daughter, was due to start her nurse's training at a hospital some hundred miles away.

O nce the funeral was over, and the various relatives had left, the three of us tiptoed around one another in the house. It felt wrong to have music blasting out, or to quarrel, both of which used to be very common occurences in the house. And I faced a dilemma. We'd booked a family holiday in Spain for the last two weeks of August, only a few weeks away, and I just didn't know what to do.

The three of us talked about it and decided that we should still go. I was having terrible problems sleeping and kept disintegrating into weeping fits, but I was also concerned that the children had something to look forward to. So, off we went. My first panic was having to drive the hire-car from the airport. My husband had always done the driving abroad because I hate it, but we survived long enough to arrive safely at the villa.

It was in a beautiful setting, close to the beach, and as we sat together on the patio and watched the sun set, I was glad we had come. There were a number of occasions in the fortnight when I thought the complete opposite, but the first night was fine. I managed to sleep well but I regretted going when I saw families together on the beach. When we had a barbecue and the kids remembered that their dad was always 83the one to get it going, and when I went down with a mystery bug for about three days, then I did wish I was back in my own home.

But the holiday did us good. When we got back, the music began to blast out again and the house began to feel more like a home than an undertaker's. It was then that Gemma announced that she wasn't going to do her nursing. I was appalled. I'd been dreading her leaving home for the first time, at this time of all times, but I didn't want her life to be more damaged by her father's death than was necessary.

It turned out that she didn't want to leave me on my own with Paul. She felt that he wouldn't support me enough, and that I needed her around too. Paul and I were able to dissuade her on that count and so with a sinking heart, just a few days later, I was driving my first-born off to the start of her new life without me. I worried about how much change she could handle in such a short period of time, but couldn't wrap her up in cotton wool as she'd tried to do to me.

So in three months our family unit of four had halved. Now it was just Paul and me. He was very moody and touchy, and I don't think I was much better. But off he went to school, and I was left at home. Day after day. I got to be very restless, cleaning furiously, and then I began to think about the future and got very low. I was only forty-four. Was I going to spend the rest of my life as a housewife? Soon Paul would be heading off to university if his A-levels were up to scratch, and then what?

I knew that financially I was very lucky. Jim had always joked about how much he was worth dead, and now I'd found out. Life assurance, endowment mortgages, pensions. If I wasn't profligate I certainly had no financial worries in the future. But what to do with the rest of my life? The image of the Merry Widow wasn't quite me.

So, in the middle of all my grief at Jim's death, a little flame of hope for the future began to burn. Before the children had been born I'd never followed a career. I'd just worked my way through a variety of secretarial jobs until I'd met Jim and we'd fallen in love. But now I wanted to work again. I didn't want to have to live off Jim's 'death money' as I saw it, for the rest of my life.

I realized that I was jealous of Gemma. She was so happy in her nurse training. But what on earth could I do? Various friends tried to persuade me to do voluntary work but I wanted more than that. I needed to find an identity, and I sensed that identity had something to do with work and earning money.

Eventually I opened a small 'natural health' centre. There wasn't one in our town and I judged there was a demand. It was an enormous risk and I had to use a lot of the money Jim had left. Everyone I talked to about it tried to dissuade me from doing it, but I'd attended various training days on running small businesses. I knew my 'admin' skills were good and I came up with a business plan that convinced the bank manager. So it opened.

It's early days yet, but our heads are above water and the accountant seems cheery enough. In a sense, what I am doing is in memory of Jim. He never took time off to relax and worked under enormous stress. This centre offers people the chance, through massage, aromatherapy and hypnosis, to de-stress themselves.

Paul was livid. He told me it would be a disaster. Then when it began to be a success he started to complain that I had changed. He told me my clothes were different, my hair was too trendy. He then accused me of trying to get another man! Nothing was further from my mind.

My relationship with Paul deteriorated to the extent that we barely talked. I also found that my friends, apart from one who came into the business as a partner, didn't phone up any more. 'You've changed so much,' one of them said. 'You're confident, busy and you've built yourself another life.' I also suspected that my married friends were deliberately keeping their husbands away from me. That hurt! Surely they knew me better than that!

But there were new friends, people who didn't know me as Jim's widow. And Paul finally came round. On the day his superb A-level results came in, he bought a huge bouquet of flowers and thanked me for showing him that hard work is one way to deal with mourning. I know it all sounds like a fairy tale, but it hasn't been at all easy. There are times when I long for the old days, when Jim was alive. And there are nights when I feel lonely and just long to have someone there to hold me and love me.

The one thing I've learned about bereavement is the need to discover new interests, or at least to get absorbed in the old ones. To go from part of a couple to a single person in one quick blow is tough. Obviously not everyone can start their own business, but I think that somehow you've got to build some sort of life on your own. I think it's also particularly hard on women. So many of us take our identity from being Mr Somebody's wife and then, when Mr Somebody dies, we've got a real struggle to find out who we are in our own right.

Vivienne's story may leave us feeling inadequate, thinking, 'It's all very well for her.' Her waying of coping was to become involved in business activity. Other people may need to be different and have space for thought and reflection as they come to terms with their loss. But it is important to find things to do which engage people's interest and help produce a feeling of being part of the human race again. To journey successfully through grief is not to emerge at the end just as before, or having forgotten what has happened. It is to emerge having lived and worked through the grief, adapting to it, and having a life which to a greater or lesser extent is enjoyable.

What that life might be depends on the circumstances, but it will depend on two major elements—having something to do, and having someone to do it with.

Firstly, everyone needs something to do. If you are bereaved and are also housebound and unwell, it may be that you can enjoy listening to the radio, or reading, or discovering a new interest— for example, writing poetry, doing crosswords, or sketching; equally you could try your hand at various crafts such as marquetry or tapestry. It may not sound like much, but if you are surrounded by the same four walls day in and day out, something to interest you is essential. If you are able to get out and about then there is a wider range of possibilities.

This first stage—thinking of things to do—is not easy, and the best way to begin is just to dream a bit. Maybe the past years, maybe many past years, have been centred around the needs of others. Now, there is just one person—you. Naturally it will feel rather empty and frightening at first, but let's move on to dreaming a bit:

☐ Is there anything which you wanted to do in the past but didn't have time for, or which other people close to you didn't enjoy?

☐ Is there anything of which you've ever thought, 'I'd love to try that but…'?

☐ Are you open to the idea of trying to learn something new?

☐ What is the one thing you would most like to do in the future?

☐ What money could be spent on it?

Any ideas? If there were one or two which were immediately dismissed with, 'But I couldn't do that at my age!' or 'What on earth would people think?' ask 'Why not?' This may be the first time in years when it's been possible to do something that only you want to do. More importantly, it may be the first time you can remember when your own needs could come first. Much of adult life is about putting other people's needs before your own, and a lifetime of doing that makes it difficult to suddenly start putting yourself first. It may even feel selfish and unchristian, but God created us with all manner of gifts and 'talents' (to use the biblical word). Perhaps this is the time to uncover some of the 'talents' that have had to be buried in the past.

Secondly, who can share these interests? Bereaved people now living on their own often feel that one of their greatest needs is for contact with other human beings. If you are in this situation, how can you go about finding that contact? How can you explore that 'dreaming' a bit further?

VOLUNTARY WORK

The range is enormous—mother and toddler groups, hospitals, old people's homes, meals on wheels, assisting people who are caring in their own homes and need a break or a helping hand, or doing something for your favourite charity. If you don't know where to start, try the town hall, the local library, the vicar or minister, or the local authority's social services department. There are also environmental organizations if you like working in the open air, and nature conservation projects frequently advertise for volunteers.

NEW INTERESTS, NEW FRIENDS

Day and evening classes are a possibility. These are organized by the local authority in schools or halls and you can do all manner of things. Although most classes begin in the early autumn, there may be some starting after Christmas or Easter. Another alternative would be a correspondence course, from the very short-term right up to a degree with the Open University.

There are also physical activities. Some groups are again organized by the local authority in leisure centres or community halls. They may be keep-fit classes of various sorts (and they are not all for bright young things in dazzling leotards—many groups are for the more mature). Or there may be bowling clubs, squash ladders, swimming groups, and so on. There may also be parkland nearby, for leisurely walks.

In addition, the local paper will have news of local events and special interest clubs. If there is no contact address given for something which catches your eye then write to the paper asking them to forward your letter. The local library will also have news of this kind.

Another way to develop new contacts is to be involved in a discussion group. Many institutions of higher education will have an extramural department that organizes talks and discussions on a range of topics for members of the public. There are also groups such as the Women's Institute or the Rotary Club. Many churches run house-groups during Lent, and there's no reason at all why they can't happen at other times of the year. If you're concerned about going out at night, talk to your vicar or minister and see if it's possible to have one that meets during the day.

If there is no general daytime activity locally for people who have time on their hands, it may be possible to start a new group—for instance, addressing the needs of newly single or bereaved people. There could be talks on coping with loneliness, cooking for one, financial advice, or home and car maintenance. Time can also be built into such meetings for people just to mingle and meet.

SOCIALIZING

One of the worst aspects of being alone is that feeling, 'I can't possibly do that on my own. I'd feel awful!' It might be going to the theatre or cinema, or something as simple as a walk, or visiting a flower show or fireworks display. The trick is organization, finding out about them long enough in advance to get other people along. It's estimated that a quarter of the homes in this country are occupied by just one person. That's an awful lot of people who might well share a sense of embarrassment about going out on their own.

If you're involved in a local church or any other community activity, why not see if you can organize a visit to the cinema or a series of local events. It need only be a few people, and all that's needed is the date for everyone to go and a time and a place to meet!

Mealtimes are another area of difficulty for people on their own. So often these used to be the occasions to swap stories of what's happened during the day, or even to talk about the weather! They might not have been the most scintillating of conversations, but if mealtime after mealtime is now passed munching snack food while gazing at the television, it may well be time for a change.

If there are others in a similar position, why not take your courage in both hands and arrange a meal together. You don't have to be a cordon bleu chef: all it needs is a simple menu. Alternatively, one person could bring along the first course, someone else the main course, and a third the dessert. All you then do is provide the table, the cutlery, and a relaxed atmosphere in which people can feel free to chat and enjoy themselves. There's nothing mysterious or new about any of this, it just needs a little courage and initiative to ask a few other people. Given the enormous courage and initiative it will already have taken to live through bereavement, many people will find they now have surprising resources!

Incidentally, in any of these activities, there is no need to worry about any social convention to balance the numbers between men and women. This is the era of the singles, and there can be a table of all men or all women, or any combination of the two that you care to name. It doesn't matter. People are there to enjoy each other's company.

A FEW MORE POSSIBILITIES

Having a pet is by no means a trivial suggestion. Cats and dogs make wonderful and affectionate companions, quite apart from bringing down the blood pressure of their owners! Walking a dog every day is excellent exercise, a great excuse to go out, and it's also a chance to meet other dog owners on the way. It may also feel better to go for walk with a dog than to do so alone.

If you enjoy singing or playing a musical instrument, it may be possible to join a choir or music group. If you enjoy the theatre, there may similarly be a local amateur dramatic society which would welcome new members.

NEW RELATIONSHIPS

If you have lost a partner then new relationships are a fundamental part of surviving the future alone. Most of us need people that we can talk to, and whose company we enjoy. But perhaps there is a prospect of a closer relationship than friendship, and maybe even a remarriage.

In some cases it can happen 'on the rebound'. Still grieving for a husband or wife, some people remarry very quickly and then regret what they have done. Sadly, such hasty marriages can lead to a great deal of unhappiness, if not divorce. But there is no rule about these things, and for people who cannot bear being on their own and need a physical, loving relationship, it can work out well.

Fiona's story

A close involvement with another person, however, no matter how soon or long after the death of a partner, does bring its own dilemmas and feelings. Fiona was widowed in her thirties when her daughters were nine and twelve. Three years after her husband's death Fiona, who had started working again as a teacher, fell in love with another teacher at the school.

*T*o begin with we just started talking over coffee or sharing a sandwich at lunchtime. We had a lot in common and enjoyed one another's company. Then one day Joseph asked if I'd like to go out for dinner one Saturday night. I felt sick! Yes I wanted to, no I didn't. Suddenly I felt like a teenager being asked on her first date. What if it was a disaster? What would I wear? What would I tell the girls? I said yes!

When I asked Cathy if she'd babysit her younger sister on the Saturday night, they both gave me the first degree. Where was I going? Who with? Their faces were a picture when I told them I was going out to dinner with a man called Joseph. Then they decided to enter into the spirit of the whole thing and tried to instruct me in the ways of the world. They decided what I should wear and what colour eye-shadow to put on. In the months after that first dinner I was to remember their enthusiasm and wonder where it had all gone.

So Joseph and I had dinner with my daughters' blessing. It was a lovely evening and I enjoyed every minute of it. Until, when Joseph dropped me off at home, he leant over and kissed me and told me how fond of me he was becoming. I froze, pushed him away and leapt out of the car. Upstairs in my bedroom I began to cry. I felt guilty, adulterous, as if I was being unfaithful to my dead husband, and frightened because I realized I wasn't sure I could love anyone else in case I lost them too and had to go all through all the heartache again.

The very next day Joseph and I talked about all of this and agreed to take things slowly. But he became more and more an important part of my life, and a less and less wanted part of the girls'. They said hurtful things. He was after my money; I was being disloyal to their dad; I was too old to get married again. When Joseph came round they were rude to him or tried to ignore him. I was at my wits' end and Joseph was hurt by it all. I felt I was losing my daughters. And then I discovered they had written to their grandparents, on their father's side, of course.

I thank God that they did. Their grandparents came to visit and over one mealtime raised the question of Joseph and me remarrying. My daughters poured out their feelings, how they were worried I was trying to replace their dad; I hesitatingly explained how we had met and how Joseph and I loved one another. Then the children's grandfather turned to them and said, 'Do you want your mother to be happy and to know that she's loved? Because if you do, then it sounds to me like Joseph's the man.' The girls looked askance, and he then went on to say, 'You know there isn't a day passes without your grandmother and me thinking about your father. But he's dead, girls, and your mother deserves some love. If she and Joseph want to marry then we wish them every happiness. All we'd ask is that you invite us to the wedding!'

And there was a wedding, six months later. Joseph and I wouldn't fix a date until we felt the girls were ready for it, but gradually they let him into their lives. We all went house-hunting together and miraculously found a home that we all felt we could live in. Our honeymoon became a family holiday and it would be good to say we all lived happily ever after. Except this is real life and not fairy-tale time. And it's fair to say we've had some tough times as well as good. It's been hard for the girls to start sharing me with someone else after they'd had my undivided attention for three years; for Joseph it's been difficult working out how best to be a stepfather to two teenage girls. And me? Well it's been stressful adapting to a new way of life and there've been times when I've heard myself saying to Joseph, 'But we don't do it that way in this family,' and then, seeing the hurt on his face, having to apologize.

But through it all our relationship has grown, and the addition of Joseph to our family was nothing other than good. And I think if you ask Joseph about all this he'll just grin and say he wouldn't have life any other way.

And that is exactly what Joseph said, but he added, 'Friends told me it would never last, and I must be mad marrying a widow and her two daughters. Well, there've been times when it's helped to be mad, but family life is always a bit crazy, isn't it?'

PUTTING THE PIECES BACK TOGETHER AGAIN

☐ With the death of someone precious, part of us dies. Ahead is a different path. Beginning that walk, we are sometimes numb and cut off from life, sometimes clothed in loneliness and blinded by hurt and anger. But with time our steps will become lighter and more confident and our despair will ease.

☐ There are no short cuts on this path, and there will be difficult times. But to get this far, we have survived—even when we never thought it possible. Inside there's a streak of survival that's got us to today and which will see us through the times ahead when we feel like giving up. Other people have made it; we can too.

11

'YOU FEEL SO HELPLESS'
Befriending the bereaved

*I avoided my best friend after her dad died. I didn't know
what to do for the best. I said I was sorry; but Alice was so
upset. I'd never seen her like it before and I felt really
embarrassed when she cried. Nobody ever tells you what
you're meant to do when a friend has gone through a
bereavement. I feel guilty when I think that I avoided her;
but I just couldn't bear seeing her so upset.*

---

*I'm West Indian, but I've lived in Britain for nearly twenty
years now. It really amazes me how much difference there
is between my culture and yours when it comes to death.
In my tradition, if somebody has lost a loved one, we go
round to the house straight away. There'll probably be a
house full of people and we'll be sad together. We'll talk
about the person who's died, telling stories about them.
There'll be people coming and going the whole time,
bringing food, offering what support they can.*

The previous chapter looked at the practical steps of rebuilding
a life after bereavement; this chapter is for everyone who wishes
they knew how best to be a friend to grieving people.

Other people's experiences can be particularly valuable here,
and they have been divided roughly into two areas. First of all
there is the period immediately after the bereavement and then
later on comes the time for more long-term support.

The first few days and weeks

Obviously a lot of what follows depends upon your relationship with the person who is grieving. Maybe it's a close friend, or an acquaintance, or perhaps a colleague at work or a neighbour. The principles are the same, however, and just require an element of sensitivity. What is appropriate for one relationship may not be exactly the same for another, but all it needs is a little thought.

Margery's story

So often we say it's the small things that matter. Margery's account of how other people reacted to, and helped her through, her husband's death shows just how supportive small actions can be.

M y husband died suddenly of a heart attack on his way home from work. Our two sons both work abroad and it wasn't possible for them to spend long with me at home, so I was very much dependent on friends to see me through.

When I first heard the news of Mike's death, the police phoned my friend Isabelle and asked her round. It was so good just to have someone there. She held my hand as I phoned the boys to tell them of their father's death. She came with me to the mortuary in the hospital, and she moved into the spare room so that I wasn't on my own at night.

Above all, she listened. I talked, over and over again, about what Mike and I had said to each other that morning when he left for work; about how we first met; about what a good husband he'd been. And every so often, something to eat or something to drink would appear in front of me and she'd urge me to at least try something!

Isabelle's husband Jonathan was a great support too. He met first Andrew, and then Simon, my sons, when they flew back home. He drove me to the undertaker's and the registrar's. There was no way I could have driven myself as I was much too shaky! He was also good at guiding me through the practicalities. There are so many practical things to do when death happens, and although I'd lost both my parents some years before, Mike had taken care of all the details.

157

But Jonathan gently took me through the things that needed to be done. It's not just the funeral arrangements, and the registration of the death. It's all the people who need to be notified. Life insurance companies, other insurance companies, banks, building societies, the Inland Revenue! There were times I felt really daunted by all the paper work, but Jonathan guided me through it!

Another thing I really treasured was the letters and cards that arrived. Some of them were from people I didn't know, mainly people Mike had worked with over the years. But it was so heart-warming to know that they cared enough to write and tell me how sorry they'd been to hear of Mike's death. One or two of them wrote short letters telling me things about Mike that they remembered with affection. It meant so much to me to hear those things about my husband which I'd never known before.

Another good thing about those first few weeks were the small gifts that neighbours delivered: fruit, flowers, bottles of wine! And my nearest neighbour who I know quite well came in the day after Mike's death and said she'd go and do some shopping for me. I remember feeling very puzzled. Why did I need some shopping doing? She asked me what I needed but I couldn't think about it at all, so she went into the kitchen and had a good look round. Two hours later the fridge was full of all sorts of useful things—just as well because it was full house over the next few days. Simon and Andrew were home; distant relatives appeared and friends dropped by.

One of the things I really valued was Isabelle saying to me that I could phone her any time of the day or night. I knew that she meant it, too, and although I tried not to disturb her at night, there were a couple of times, about one in the morning, when I just wanted another human being to speak to. So I phoned and true to her word, she got up and came round, letting me talk and cry until I was ready to sleep.

When I think about what I've just said it makes it sound like people were really supportive. And they were, don't get me wrong. But there were some people in the street who honestly did look the other way when they saw me out walking. And I found it infuriating when other people asked me if I was feeling better now! I'd lost my husband, how on earth did they expect me to feel?

But overall, because bereavement is such an isolating experience and so knocks you for six, it means that all contact with other people *becomes very important. It makes you realize that the things we normally worry about like the recession, and whether or not to get a new car, are nothing when compared to the way we need one another.*

I was so grateful when somebody would stop and talk to me if I was out in the front garden doing some weeding, or if somebody smiled at me in the supermarket. I also found I was much more sensitive to how other people might be feeling, and so occasionally when I was walking in the park, if I saw a bench with an older person sitting there on their own, I'd sit down beside them and begin a conversation. More often than not it turned out they were now on their own after a bereavement, and we'd have a really good time of sharing with one another.

So, if other people want to know how best to deal with the bereaved, on the basis of my experience I'd say:

1) Show that you care. A letter or card can mean so much!

2) Offer your help in practical ways. Don't ask, is there anything I can do? Be specific. Can I cut the grass/run you to the shops/ accompany you somewhere? Just remember that making decisions about everyday things is actually very difficult when you're in a state of shock, so sometimes it's a case of just thinking about what might need to be done and doing it!

3) Don't offer to help if you don't really want to. There is nothing worse than taking someone up on an offer and then feeling that they'd really rather that you hadn't.

4) Don't worry about upsetting the bereaved person by talking about the person who's died. Nearly all of us want to talk about the loved one we've lost, and will be grateful for the opportunity to do so. If we cry, there's no need to be embarrassed, just don't try to dismiss our pain. Let us express it, and you needn't worry about finding the right words to say. All we need is for you to be there and to listen.

Margery's advice has been echoed by many other bereaved people I've heard from. But is there a specifically Christian input? Is there an additional element which faith can add when we are wondering about how to support someone who is grieving?

Of course, there is the Christian imperative to love and care for one another and this can be very concrete. But many people who would not call themselves Christian are just as good at caring, sometimes better.

So is there something which is specifically Christian? There is, and it is to do with an understanding about the very nature of life itself. Christians believe that life is a gift from God, and that at death the soul returns to be with God. Through the life and atoning death of Jesus, and as evidenced by his resurrection, they believe there is a life after death. (At this point the different Christian traditions differ in emphasis.)

But Christians also believe that the selfless example of Jesus' life was the way of God on earth. Moreover, Jesus no more wanted us flamboyantly to proclaim our religion than he did the Pharisee on the street corner outside the synagogue.

If we are about to visit someone who is newly bereaved, we therefore need to be sensitive about what we say by way of Christian comfort, as opposed to what we do. The most fervent believer will still feel pain at the loss of someone they loved and it would be catastrophic and totally unchristian to urge them, 'Be thankful, because the person you are mourning has gone to be with the Lord.' Jesus didn't say what a lucky old fellow Lazarus was to be with God; he wept. For the sense of loss remains, and feelings of grief are a normal, healthy human reaction.

This is not to say we must never talk of our faith, but we must be aware that sometimes it is easier to try to introduce optimism and cheer than it is just to feel the weight of someone else's pain. We must try to be conscious of who it is we are trying to help— the person who is grieving, or ourselves. By that I mean, are we trying to ease a situation because it will help the other person, or really because, deep down, we will feel more comfortable? After all, hearing another's distress is actually a harrowing experience.

These are quite hard thoughts to take on board, but just think how many times all of us do it? How often have we asked someone how they are, expecting to hear the normal answer of 'Fine, thank you!' only to hear instead 'Well I'm really worried I'm about to lose my job,' or words to that effect. Can we, hand on heart, say that we have never in such a situation said, 'I'm sure you'll be fine!' and then changed the topic of discussion?

We all do it, and it is particularly true with bereavement.

Getting close to another's grief can stir up all sorts of feelings in ourselves. We may be reminded of our own feelings of loss, sometimes from years ago. Or we may be reminded of our own vulnerability and mortality. That can be unnerving, and it is probably why we are sometimes guilty of trying to avoid such situations—it is, after all, a perfectly normal response to avoid pain. But it is not at all helpful for the person who is left to feel either that they are being ignored, or that their grief is being denied. We need to be sensitive to what what we're doing and saying, and why we might be saying it.

But the other side of sharing someone else's pain, is being able to detach ourselves from it. It is possible to get so involved that we become physically and emotionally drained. Jesus frequently needed to withdraw and spent long hours away from those to whom he ministered. We, too, need the opportunity to talk about our own reactions to someone with a sympathetic, listening ear. It means that after sharing sadness with the bereaved person, we ourselves need time to talk with a friend or partner about how we're feeling about it all. It needn't be a heavy session, but it will be a necessary escape valve for some bottled-up feelings.

Bill's story

Sarah and Bill lost their baby, George, when he was just four days old and they were amazed at how differently people reacted to them.

There were two doctors that we'd seen on a daily basis. The younger one seemed embarrassed by our grief. She came over and said she was sorry, and then scuttled off and never came near us again. But the older one, the registrar, actually cried when he came to talk with us. He was obviously upset and didn't mind us knowing it. He stroked George's head, saying something like, 'Sorry George, one day we'll be able to save chaps like you, but not yet.' That meant so much to us, knowing that he wasn't an unfeeling automaton, and that he too was affected by George's death.

Once we were back home it was difficult to know what to tell people. I mean, for instance, people at work. As far as most of my colleagues knew I was off on a few days of paternity leave, so I dreaded going back in. In the end I asked my boss to tell one or two individuals, and I was sure the office gossips would soon ensure that everyone else knew pretty rapidly.

The day I walked back in, the whole office went quiet for a few seconds and then people busied themselves. Sitting on my desk was a lovely card, signed by them all, which just simply stated: 'We cannot find words to say how sorry we are.' A close colleague came by, and his obvious distress removed the last vestige of the protective shell that I'd had to don to walk through the door. The tears started again, but not for long, and afterwards I felt better, and was ready to tackle some of the in-tray that had piled up in my absence.

At Christmas time Sarah and I sent out a Christmas letter, which we'd thought long and hard about sending, but finally felt it was the right thing to do. What we wanted to say to our friends and family was this:

As Christmas approaches, and people everywhere gather to celebrate the birth of the Christ child, we ask you to pray for all people like ourselves who this Christmas will be reminded of the empty crib in their own homes. It won't be an easy time for any of us.

If George had lived he would have been six months old now, and not a day passes when we don't think of him and what he might have been doing. But it wasn't to be. His heart was too badly damaged for him to live, and we firmly believe that he is now safe with his heavenly Father.

But as well as asking for your prayers, we would like to thank you for all the messages of care and support you've sent over the last months. And we'd like to say, don't be afraid to talk to us of George and of his death. You won't upset us any more than we already are, and we value the opportunity to know that he is not forgotten.

Equally we like to hear news of your children and what they are up to. So many people have begun to tell us something about a child of theirs and then said, "Oh, sorry, that was unfeeling of me." But do talk to us of children and their antics. We don't want you to censor them out of your conversations with us. We're learning to live with our loss, not by avoiding it, but facing it.

We wanted to write that letter because it was obvious that some of our friends had difficulty in knowing what to say to us, and we wanted *to make it clear how we felt about that. Most people were really pleased that we'd written it, but Sarah's mother was appalled. She thought we ought to be forgetting about George now, and getting on with having another baby! But at least we were now able to talk about all of that with her.*

When you read both Bill and Margery's accounts of what helped support them through bereavement and the things they themselves did, you can begin to see how you might help someone who is grieving. They are simple things really, but they are all based on letting that person know that you care. In summary they would probably read something like this:

DON'T IGNORE THE DEATH
Avoidance seems to be a classic British reaction to bereavement, and is one thing which many bereaved people have said causes them untold pain. If you can't bear facing someone, at least drop a note or a card into the post.

BE PRACTICAL
You can show you care by all means of practical support: mowing the lawn, doing the shopping, helping clear up or running errands.

BE READY TO LISTEN
The only rule is to allow people to say what they want to say, in the way they want to say it, and to be attentive. That's what listening is really about.

REMEMBER THAT GRIEF IS A LENGTHY PROCESS
Support needs to be offered not just in the first few days and weeks, but over months and even years.

Support in the longer term
Usually, everyone rallies round in an emergency, and the same is true of a death which affects a friend, colleague or family member. But after a few weeks the initial urgency is lost and people get caught up in their own lives again and begin to

forget about the person who they have been trying to help and support. For the person who was bereaved this can herald a time of isolation. All around them are people who are going about ordinary everyday things as if nothing had changed and yet they themselves are living with irrevocable change—the loss of someone who was very important to them, whom they loved. Grief is not a passing phase. It's there to be lived with and faced until adjustment is made. In the case of a major bereavement, such as the death of a spouse or child, it can be as long as two years or more.

Time-scales are not particularly helpful, however. It is enough to know that grieving is a long process and support should not be withdrawn after a few weeks.

The greatest need for long-term support from others is, of course, after the loss of a partner. The widow or widower has not only lost a husband or wife, but the life that they lived together and the support that they gave to one another. Beginning to face the future for such people means learning to live without the support that marriage gave them and, in many cases, learning to live alone.

Earlier in this chapter, Margery talked of the support she had in the early days after her husband's death. Three years after his death was she still in need of support?

I don't like to think of it as support, but do I need the time and friendship of other people? Oh yes, most definitely. I've got used to living on my own but if I had to go more than a couple of days without seeing anyone I can have a good conversation with, I'd go mad!

It's the loneliness that's the worst thing of all. We'd been married for thirty-three years when Mike died, and during that time I think I spent only a handful of nights without him, so even though some nights we'd just sit in front of the television and not talk much at all, at least he was there! Now there are a lot of evenings when I come back late afternoon and know that I'm on my own till the morning. It makes the evenings seem really long. There are nights I look at my watch and can't believe it's only nine o'clock. It feels like it ought to be midnight!

That's why I love invitations to go out at night. Not for anything special but just to spend the evening with others. Isabelle and Jonathan have me round about once a week, and we have a bite of supper and play scrabble. I'm always wary about being a burden to them, but they keep saying I'm not. I'd hate it if ever they thought, 'Oh no, we'd better have Margery round again this week.' That would be awful.

I go to our parish church every Sunday, but they don't have much going on during the week—not at night, anyway. It's OK if you're a Brownie or a Boy Scout, but I'm a bit old for that! Sometimes I think the church forgets there are lots of people on their own.

I've recently become good friends with another two widows I met through CRUSE, the charity that works with bereaved people. Now and again we'll visit the cinema or the theatre, and we often meet for coffee. But sometimes I long to be part of a family again. Once a year each of my sons comes home with his wife and children and, apart from the fact I love seeing them, you've no idea how different it feels when you go out. I feel like I actually 'belong' to someone. I suppose that sounds like an odd thing to say, but when we go for a walk along the river, and we pass other people, I can look them in the eye and smile and say hello, and usually they smile back. But when I'm on my own and pass someone, sometimes I don't feel safe. And other times when I do greet them, they look taken aback and then look away.

Another thing I'd say to people who've got friends who are widowed is that sometimes you've got to exert a bit of gentle pressure. I've always been a cheerful person and enjoyed getting out and about, but about a year or so after Mike's death I just couldn't be bothered to do anything. It felt like too much effort to get ready to go out, and I'd be scared of meeting new people or going into new situations.

Looking back I suppose I was suffering from a mild depression, but it was Isabelle who kept persevering. She'd phone up and ask me to do something like come round for a meal on Saturday night. And when I'd hesitate, or think of some excuse, she'd find a way round it. She'd come and pick me up and then when I got there I enjoyed myself, but it was just a bit of an effort getting me there!

I can see how easy it is to slip into the habit of saying 'no' to things and then people give up on you, and never ask you to anything. Fortunately, Isabelle wasn't good at taking 'no' for an answer. But she didn't bully me, either. I think she could sense that there were times when I should be on my own, and times when a bit of company was all I needed.

Drawing from Margery's experience, and others in similar situations, there seem to be several ways to be a good friend in the longer term.

SHARE YOUR TIME

It's always hard adapting to change, whatever the reason. A major bereavement creates a void that only a long period of adjustment can fill. During and after that time, it's good to have friends who won't demand scintillating company, but who will let you talk about what you're feeling without getting embarrassed or trying to change the subject. So if you can offer time, a warm welcome, a listening ear or even just another brain on a crossword puzzle, then you will be of help.

It's good, too, if you knew the person who died. Don't be afraid to talk about the past because the sharing of memories is often welcomed by the grieving.

COAX, BUT DON'T BULLY

There's only a thin dividing line between these two. There is nothing worse than someone trying to force another person to do something they just don't want to do. Equally, many bereaved people may need a little coaxing if you're thinking of including them in an outing or a meal. The difficulty is knowing when to accept that the answer really is a 'no'. Just try and be sensitive.

URGE PATIENCE

After the first few weeks some bereaved people talk of making major life changes—selling the family home, or moving away to a completely new part of the country. These are such life-changing decisions that they need to be made with much thought, and not in the emotional aftermath of a recent bereavement.

If you can, urge patience and recommend that the decision is left until some agreed period of time has elapsed—such as six months, or a year.

BE ALERT

There may be some practical ways to help. Immediately after the death you may have looked for things to do, but perhaps you have now stopped because time has moved on. Yet there may still be things that you can do.

A hand with some decorating might well be useful, or a bit of car maintenance or even some gardening. It may well be that the offer of another pair of hands prompts the completion of a chore that would otherwise have been left.

Making tedious telephone calls seems to be a particular ordeal for those who have been bereaved—for instance, to find an estimate for some piece of house maintenance or to ask the gas or electricity services to rectify a fault. Perhaps you might ring round for them. Once such jobs are completed, it can add a real boost to morale.

Writing Christmas cards is another very difficult task for those who have lost a partner or a child. You can't write someone's cards for them, but simply being present may be a comfort, and you could offer to address envelopes or help in some other way.

DON'T SLINK AWAY

If you really do want to support a friend through bereavement, try to be honest. If you find that demands are being made on you that you are not happy about, then try to say so. Not nastily, or angrily, but sensitively. It might be more comfortable to put the answering machine on for the next fortnight and be unavailable, but the bereaved person will be left a bit 'at sea', wondering if they've caused offence in any way.

It's fairer to say to them, 'I'm ever so sorry, but I'm afraid it's getting a bit difficult when you phone every night at midnight. It would be fine at about nine, but if it's the nights that are hard perhaps you'd let me help you find other people to talk to?'

If you do find yourself looking for excuses to avoid your friend's company, ask yourself why. Is it because you find your friend's conversation depressing, even boring? Perhaps there's a little voice saying, 'I wish she'd cheer up, she ought to be getting over it by now!' Maybe it's because you feel in need of a bit of light relief. After all, a day by day reminder of mortality can be a bit tough on anyone.

Nobody would condemn you if you were to feel like this. It's perfectly understandable. See if you can find light relief elsewhere: other friends, a swim, a good book, even a favourite television programme. This way you will find more energy to listen sympathetically. Above all, don't feel guilty. It is very important not to confuse your very real need for a break with a reaction against your friend. You may have to go on supporting and befriending for a long time and it would be dreadful if you were to do this with resentment in your heart, or if you were to 'extricate' yourself by becoming inexplicably busy or unavailable.

THE NEED FOR PROFESSIONAL HELP

Occasionally the normal process of bereavement can 'get stuck', or depressive illness can occur. The difficulty is knowing when professional help is required. Professionals such as GPs sometimes have difficulty in recognizing serious depression, so how can you tell the warning signs?

On the one hand you cannot be expected to diagnose when a friend's grief might need more help than you and others can give. On the other hand, if you are not alert to it, who else will be?

If you are beginning to get concerned, you might try contacting one of the organizations listed at the back of this book to see if they have any groups or 'listening' services in your area of the country. They have enormous experience, and if your friend were to contact them it might be all that is required. Sometimes the opportunity to talk with other people who have gone through a similar experience can be extremely uplifting, odd though that may seem.

Alternatively, you may notice symptoms of depression—difficulty in sleeping, early wakening, loss of appetite, poor concentration, talk of suicide. Try then to encourage the seeking of professional help. If necessary, go along too. The observation of a friend can help underline the seriousness of symptoms.

Visiting a counsellor who specializes in bereavement or seeking psychiatric help can be extremely beneficial. Obviously not everyone needs such help, but at times it is necessary. If it is felt necessary by the GP, be supportive. There is still a stigma attached to seeking such help, but it should be no different to consulting any other specialist. Whatever you do, don't back off now. Your support and friendship are even more critical.

YOU FEEL SO HELPLESS

☐ There is no mystery or special skill required where supporting the bereaved is concerned. The key contribution you have to make is your friendship, your time and your common sense. Use your eyes and ears to see what might be needed in practical terms, and make yourself available.

☐ Initially, don't wait to be asked to help or worry about intruding. Equally, don't ask questions which require some kind of decision. Grief begins with a state of shock and it is very difficult to think logically or to make decicions.

☐ Longer term, remember that grieving lasts a long time and can leave problems of loneliness or a sense of uselessness. Just be there as a true friend—to listen, to encourage, and to let someone know they haven't been forgotten. The Bible calls it 'lovingkindness'.

12

STRUGGLING TO MAKE SENSE OF IT ALL

I was devastated when my son Gordon died four years ago. He was just sixteen. Even now I can see no purpose in it whatsoever. If I have learnt anything at all from the despair and agony, it is that love is very precious indeed.

═══════════

I was very close to my grandmother. I'd spent much of my childhood with her, and when I moved away from home I phoned her regularly and visited when I could. But she began to get frail, and was forced to move into sheltered housing. Only two months later, she died. Obviously I was sad she'd gone, but I could see it was right. She'd said she was ready to die, and she was!

═══════════

I was with my wife, Elspeth, when she died. I'm not a particularly religious man, and I've always felt that this life was all that we had. And yet when she slipped away, so peacefully, I had a sense that she had moved on. It's very difficult to explain, but it really made me think that there is another world beyond this one.

═══════════

The reason that the title of this chapter is 'Struggling to make sense of it all' is because that is all we can ever attempt to do.

There are things that we have hunches about. We might say we have a faith. If we're really keen, we might read theological text books! But none of this gives us any ultimate proof. How do we begin to find answers that satisfy us when we ask why we are born, why we die, and whether there is a life after death?

Some people find wisdom within one of the different branches of Christianity, or other world religions. Others turn to philosophy. Spiritualists would say that they have proof of the human spirit's survival beyond death (although there is something strange about trying to make sense of life and death by a process which is fixed on a 'world' which only the spiritualist can see), and in recent years there has been a great deal of interest in near-death experiences. Or perhaps we shouldn't be asking questions, as long as we have faith?

Maria's story

Maria asked questions and did find partial answers through the suffering and death of her husband, Tom. She is a lively, dynamic woman in her forties, and Tom died at home of a particularly virulent cancer. Their three teenage children were all at home during this time.

*T*om *had just turned thirty-eight when it was discovered that a mole on his back was a malignant melanoma. Both of us were shocked but we didn't tell the children about it because we believed the doctors who reassured us that it had been caught quickly enough.*

We thanked God that we'd been encouraged to seek medical help so quickly, and we joked about it as 'an intimation of mortality'—a timely reminder that none of us is here for ever. But what we didn't joke about was how much it had reminded us that we loved and needed each other. Those first few weeks after we'd heard that Tom should be 'in the clear' were like a second honeymoon. Our loving and being loved was better than ever before because we knew each other so well and had shared so much throughout our marriage.

We promised we would never take each other for granted any more, and started going to church again. When the children were younger we used to go every week as a family, but gradually the habit had slipped and somehow God had been squeezed out of our busy schedule. But Tom's brush with cancer jolted us, and together we decided that it was time to bring the spiritual sharing back into our life together. The children were very suspicious when Tom and I announced that we were going to church and they were all welcome to come with us. There was a unanimous cry of, 'No!', and then Sarah the youngest asked us why we were starting to go again. It was the time to come clean with them.

It took a while to reassure them that their dad was going to be OK but eventually they said they believed us, and Sarah decided she'd come too, so that she could ask God to make sure that her dad was going to be all right. Sarah was ten at this time. The other two—Fiona was thirteen and George was fifteen—considered themselves atheists and scoffed at her, but Sarah, true to her word, joined us.

I enjoyed going back to church, and found a joy and comfort there. It was like returning to a familiar place, and after, I felt that this was where I was meant to be—that seemed strange! Tom, too, had been really glad that we had gone, and said that in a funny sort of way he was glad the melanoma had been discovered. 'It's reminded me of the real priorities in life,' he said.

The next few months were idyllic. It was so good to be alive. Everything seemed to come together and Tom and I allowed ourselves to reach out to God again, and enjoyed our rediscovered faith.

Then Tom became ill. He lost his energy and appetite, and started to get abdominal pain. We prayed that it was something like appendicitis, but deep down we feared the worst.

We were right. The malignant melanoma had not been caught as early as the doctors had thought. Tom's cancer had spread.

We were devastated. Tom began all manner of rigorous medical treatments and we found ourselves asking, 'Why?' Surely the initial diagnosis had been the jolt that God had wanted, to bring us back to him. What more could be gained from this torment?

One night I went through what I can only call 'the long dark night of the soul'. Tom was back in hospital, the children were asleep, and the house was quiet. I couldn't settle. Inside a voice kept saying, 'A God of love wouldn't do this to you!', and I couldn't answer it. Yet I needed to know that God was for real, that he did really love us. I looked at the evidence against: pain, suffering, war, starvation, poverty, loneliness. *The world became a very bleak place indeed. But then I realized that so many of these nightmare situations were man-made. God hadn't caused them.*

But the nagging voice persisted, *'If Tom dies, after all your prayers for him to live, isn't that a sign there is no God?'* And for a time the 'voice' won. I was desolate at the thought of having to live without Tom. I felt cold and lonely and deeply afraid. No, it wasn't possible, it was too much to bear. I began to cry—with self-pity, with fear, with hopelessness. *'God, if you're really there, if you're really with us in all of this, show me!'* I prayed it over and over again, but I found no answer.

Every hour the clock chimed, proclaiming the relentless march of time. Still I had no answer. I tried to read my Bible, but couldn't. I remembered life before Tom; the day we met; our wedding day; the children's birth. What had it all been for?

And then, just before dawn, the birdsong began. Noisily a chorus announced the dawn of a new day. I pulled the curtains back, and watched as the dark sky slowly began to lighten. There was no sun to see, but it was there. Yet again night had turned to day. And it was only then that my panic began to recede. I felt a part of a continuum of time. Since the world began, millions of years ago, every day had begun this way. Generation after generation had been born, lived and then died. And Tom and I, and the children, were a part of a living generation for only a relatively short time. Our death, I realized, is a part of God's plan for the world. Just as the sun keeps rising, we need to die, ready to experience whatever lies beyond death.

My answer had begun! Intuitively I knew that Tom was going to die, soon. But I found comfort in accepting that death is part of life. I don't believe that God makes bad things happen to us. Tom's cancer probably had more to do with man's destruction of the planet through damaging the ozone layer, than with a deliberate intention on the part of God to strike Tom down. I was prepared to trust God in whatever lay ahead.

Some of our new Christian friends told us that all we had to do was pray harder, or visit a Christian healer or repent, and Tom would be healed. God, they said, was waiting to show us his power in a remarkable way. Now, years on, I realize that it was easier for them to say such things, and then blame Tom and me when things got worse, than it was to hear our pain and confusion about what was happening to Tom.

Two people helped us at that time. One was Liz, our vicar's wife, and the other was the hospital chaplain. Liz struggles daily with chronic pain from arthritis and, in the hours that she spent with Tom and me, I sensed that her own pain made it possible for her to share ours. When we asked the question 'why?', she never rushed in to answer. She just talked of the half-answers she had discovered to her own question of 'why?'

The chaplain helped me to understand and accept that half-answers are probably all that I could expect in my lifetime. Life would be different if we knew exactly what happened after death, or knew that we could manipulate God into doing what we wanted, just by praying hard enough. Where would the mystery be, and what would be the point of faith?

As I'd known intuitively, Tom's treatment did not work. There was nothing further that could be done for him other than to relieve his pain. Tom came home to die.

The chaplain urged us to pray for the fruits of the Spirit: love, joy, peace, patience, kindness, goodness, faithfulness, self-control, gentleness. But he also urged us to be honest with God about all that we felt—to throw all of our confusion and hurt and anger at him. And it was there, despite my acceptance of death as a part of life and as a part of God's plan for us. We love, and therefore we are bound to feel pain when we are separated by death.

Our daily prayer was that, as a family living with the knowledge that we were soon to lose Tom, the Holy Spirit would work within us. We told God that we did not understand why this was happening to us, but asked him to take our confusion and pain and to help us in our despair.

When I look back now I can see that it was as if we had moved beyond words and that all of our lives were part of that prayer. When I washed Tom, when he was too weak to do it for himself, I felt a giving from my heart. It became an act of such tenderness and love that I just know God was ministering to Tom, through me. I know it sounds daft, but as I touched Tom it felt sacramental—an outward and visible sign of an inward giving of grace. As if Tom was being bathed not just with soap and water, but with the very love of God himself.

We all became very close as a family. The two resident atheists who at first exhibited enormous anger—and quite rightly so—at their father's terminal illness, mellowed and had long conversations with their father about what life was all about. They became more thinking, caring people who value life. Being so close to their father during his last weeks, and being present when he died, touched them deeply. Together we witnessed the transformation in Tom as he approached death, and saw his peacefulness.

My own perception of life altered with Tom's death. It was like everything I accepted intellectually, I now knew was for real. I could see, three days before Tom died, that his body could take very little more. It had become so helpless and emaciated that I could only pray it wouldn't be much longer. Mercifully, effective drug treatments meant that Tom wasn't in pain and, though he slept a lot, when he woke Tom, the true Tom, was strong and glad that he was soon to be free.

Tom was ready to die, and we were ready for him to go. We had all said goodbye in our different ways, and not one of us could wish for him to live longer than necessary in that poor, ravaged body. So the night he died, we were all there at the bedside, talking to him, holding him. He was in a coma by this time, of course, and his breathing had become very laboured. As the four of us sat there, keeping our vigil of love, I was struck by the parallel to the children's birth.

Then it had been me who laboured, and Tom who encouraged, as my body struggled to bring new life into the world. Now that same new life, about to grow into adulthood, watched and waited, as their father was born into the next world. We were there supporting him as he journeyed on to whatever lies beyond death.

That realization was one of those moments when heaven and earth become one. Captured in that moment was the meaning of life itself, and I finally understood how transitory this world really is and sensed the presence of eternity. At the moment of Tom's death there was such a sense of God and the whole communion of saints with us, offering comfort but there to welcome Tom, that I cried with ecstasy.

I rarely talk about this because it's very difficult to find the words to describe such an overwhelming feeling. Through Tom's death I have learned so much about life and our place within God's purpose. I'm not afraid of death any more, and although I miss Tom enormously,

I'm convinced that one day we'll be reunited.

Knowing what I know now, would I go through it again? Of course not! I'm only human, and if I could wave a magic wand then my wish would be that Tom hadn't become ill and died, and that we were still together as a family. But life just isn't like that. It moves on relentlessly. Were Tom still alive we'd still have to have coped with the children finding their independence and leaving home. Nothing remains the same for ever.

And that, for me, is the meaning of life. We might think we've built a safe cocoon, and that cocoon can be wealth, achievement, health, even faith; but it isn't inviolable. When all our defences are down we are all vulnerable people who need one another, and who need to feel loved. At the heart of that love is God.

Maria's moving account illustrates how death itself can be seen positively. This is not to say that there will be no grief and no sense of loss. Such feelings are inevitable and, indeed, healthy. The positive element is that, with the words of St Paul in the first letter to the Corinthians, it is possible to say:

*F*or this perishable nature must put on the imperishable, and this mortal nature must put on immortality. When the perishable puts on the imperishable, and the mortal puts on immortality, then shall come to pass the saying which is written: Death is swallowed up in victory. O Death, where is thy victory? O Death, where is thy sting? (1 Corinthians 15:53–55)

But do we move on? Does the mortal put on the immortal? Even without faith it is difficult to believe that this life is all that we have. The universe, the planets, the sheer complexity and variety of plant, animal and human life, make it harder to believe that it all came into being through an accidental 'Big Bang', than to accept that God, the divine designer, called it all into being.

With faith added to the equation, we can begin to build up a picture of a real purpose to our lives. From the very first stirring of life, when we were being nurtured in our mother's womb, a pattern for our lives was laid. The pattern determined whether our hair would be blond or black, whether we were geniuses or gentle plodders, and it put into place our very own unique, genetic make-up. One more divine original!

None of this proves that there is anything after death. It merely points to the complexity of life, and seems reasonable evidence for assuming that as we don't understand all that goes on in this world, how can we possibly prove there is nothing beyond it?

Christians believe that Jesus lived, died and rose again. Throughout the centuries they have disputed quite how this happened: was it a physical resurrection or a spiritual one? We need to turn to the New Testament, to the accounts of Christ's resurrection, to seek to understand what those accounts mean.

There is no doubt that Jesus' followers believed something momentous had happened. Why would a group of dejected, defeated Jewish people, whose messiah had just been put to death in a most public and humiliating way, be transformed into a movement of energy and vitality? The reason was that the defeated followers said that Jesus had returned from the dead. It could have been mass hysteria or hallucination, of course, but there are several accounts of resurrection appearances to different people at different times. To Mary Magdelene at the tomb; to the disciples when they were gathered together, hiding; to Thomas, some eight days later, again when the disciples were together; to Simon Peter, and some of the other disciples when they were fishing at the Sea of Tiberias; and to Cleopas and Simon walking on the road to Emmaus. This last account is of two men being joined by a stranger. They tell him about what had happened to Jesus, including reports that his body had gone from the tomb. The stranger stays with them and later, when he breaks bread with them, they realize that they, too, have seen the risen Christ. Full of excitement, they race back to Jerusalem.

For many people these accounts are convincing evidence that Jesus survived beyond death. They do not tell us what that survival is like, what happens in heaven, or what it all means. But they do tell us that life is more than death.

Of course, it may all be wishful thinking. None of us likes to think that we will cease to exist. Throughout history, society after society has spoken and planned for an afterlife. Egyptian pharoahs were buried with the things they would require. The spirits of ancestors have been revered in many tribal cultures, and religions throughout the world have tried to make sense of death. Perhaps it is that deep within each one of us there is an instinct that life persists in some form beyond death. It might be wishful thinking, or it might be a perception of truth. Fear of death versus purpose in death? It's the paradox in which we are forced to live.

If, however, what happens beyond death really is still confined to the world of faith or the paranormal, can we draw any insight from life this side of the grave?

Birth into this world offers us a life experience in which to learn, to grow, and to develop in body, mind and spirit. We form relationships and we learn to love. We are inspired by acts of enormous heroism and self-sacrifice; and we are appalled by the inhumanity of man to man. We may be moved to creativity or bored by tedium. We may father and mother new life. We may make our path through life in other ways. But just as nature lives through the four seasons, from spring to summer, from autumn to winter, it seems right that human beings too are part of the cycle of life and death. No wonder the words of the book of Ecclesiastes find resonance with so many people:

F or everything there is a season, and a time for every matter under heaven:
a time to be born, and a time to die;
a time to plant, and a time to pluck up what is planted;
a time to kill, and a time to heal . . .

The problem with this passage comes when people die before the right season, that is, long before their three-score years and ten. As so many of the accounts in this book have shown, death brings grief and sorrow in its wake, and some deaths just seem tragic and outrageous. There is too much overwhelming loss to write happily of victory through death. It would be triumphalist and unfeeling. And it is impossible to see any purpose in needless famine, or any victory in the deaths of thousands of innocent people through war.

There is a lot of physical, emotional and mental pain in life. The new testament of Jesus, however, is not just about the resurrection but also about Jesus who was born as the Son of Man. In Jesus' life on earth we see God caring deeply about the things which make human beings hurt—sickness, being a social outcast, being lost. In his life, his ministry and his death, Jesus shows us a God who is with us in our pain, and who knows our being at its very worst.

The message of Jesus is a simple one. Heal the sick, accept the outcast and find the lost. Or, in other words, love one another, just as your father in heaven loves you. On this precept is built the kingdom of God.

Time after time, though, that message is ignored, and some of the most tragic sequences in human history have resulted—not from a vengeful God determined to punish his erring people, but from our own wilfulness and selfishness. In a fallen world marred by inhumanity and injustice, even when it is transformed through love and compassion, how is it possible to claim that death has not won?

For some people the question remains unanswerable. For others, their experience and their faith (as in Maria's account earlier) tell them that this life is the channel for the next. Not an easy exit, but a labour of love which delivers to God our soul and our spirit, shaped and refined by our dealings with others and moulded by a lifetime's experience, no matter how short or long.

This understanding of our lives as the place where we grow spiritually before entering the kingdom of Heaven may not take account of the deaths of babies, young children and those who have had relatively little opportunity to develop. One answer is that our own time-scales and human perspectives are not those of God. We do not know, and in this lifetime can never know, the exact purposes of God and the whole of his creation.

But in our day-to-day living, and in our relationships with those we love and who love us, we can value the life that we do have, knowing that we cannot hold on to it for ever. In the Sermon on the Mount, Jesus urges us not to worry about tomorrow; each day has troubles enough of its own. 'Live each day as if your last' may seem a tall order, but it has a legitimate heritage!

Marion's story

Marion's mother, Beth, was widowed during the Second World War. At that time Marion was just three years old and so, as long as she could remember, her only parent had been her mother. There were no brothers or sisters and when she thought back, Marion could see how close she and her mother were.

It was only when Marion married a man she had met at the factory where she worked, that she moved away from the home she'd lived in all those years.

I *knew Mum was heartbroken that I'd gone, although she was glad that I was finally marrying someone. (Not that I went far because Bill and I moved into a flat just a few streets away from her.) I used to worry about her, and how she was going to cope. But she seemed to adapt quite well. She always came to us for Sunday lunch, or we'd go to hers, and I popped round when I could.*

Although she was well into her sixties by this stage, the next thing I knew she became a home help for the social services. When I asked her whether this was a wise thing to do, I'll never forget what she said. 'Marion, all my life I've had someone to care for. First it was my own mum, and then your dad, God rest their souls, and then it was you. But you've got your own home now, and after a lifetime of having someone to look after, I can't stop now.'

Bill and I soon had our first baby, a little daughter, and life continued much as before—apart from the interrupted nights. Mum loved Sara and spoiled her something rotten, and it made her day if I asked her to take Sara for a couple of hours while I went shopping.

It was round about this time that the council stopped all their home help for cost reasons, but though Mum was a bit put out to begin with, she'd found an elderly neighbour or two who she could do errands for, and seemed quite happy.

It must have been the year Mum turned seventy-four that I suddenly realized she had aged. Up until then I could have sworn that she'd looked the same for ages, but that year she began to look frail. She walked awkwardly, forgot things, and she began to get moody in a way I'd never seen before. Even Sara, who adored her grandma, said that she was no fun any more.

I worried a lot about it, but Bill wasn't very sympathetic. In the end I talked to the family doctor about it and he said he'd drop by on Mum. He phoned the next day and asked me to come in to talk to him. Basically his message was that he'd been shocked by the deterioration in Mum and he was concerned that she wasn't able to look after herself any more. Had I thought about her coming to live with me?

I might as well have suggested that she go to live on the moon. She was livid. That doctor had no right to poke his nose in where it had no business, I think was how she described it. So I left her in her own home, visiting at least twice a day. But then one day I called round and she didn't answer the door. She was still in bed, ashen white, and only barely conscious.

It was at the hospital that I was advised either to take her into my own home or find sheltered accommodation for her. There was something wrong with the blood supply to her brain and she kept passing out. There was nothing they could do for her. And so, after a few days, Mum came home with me. She cried, she sulked and she refused to come out of her room. She just wasn't my mum any more, and it wasn't long before this hostile stranger was causing rows between Bill and me. Bill begged me to find a home for her, but I couldn't. All my life Mum had been there for me, and now I wanted to be there for her.

It was all so incredibly sad. This lovely person deep down, who cared for so many people in her lifetime, now needed the care of others, but she hated it. She couldn't settle to a quiet life, and rather than knit, or read, or watch television, she just seemed to get angry that she couldn't do what she wanted to.

Eventually I couldn't bear it any longer and confronted her. This time, instead of telling me to go away, she cried. Out it all came, and I realized how difficult it was for fiercely independent people to admit their own needs. She told me how she hated not having the strength to do things that she used to do, and admitted that she was afraid that the next time she passed out, that she would never wake up again.

I don't think there's anything in life which prepares you for the time when you see a parent become fragile and almost child-like. And then when they reveal their own deep-seated fears, and they are no longer strong and protective of you, it is dreadful.

So Mum and me sat there on her bed, both crying. Silently I prayed that I would find the words to comfort her. I was completely out of my depth and had no real idea of what to say. So I just told her how much I loved her and how much she'd given me over the years, and that now I'd like to return some of that love by caring for her.

We got very close again then. She became much easier to be with, and I tried to be sensitive. Making sure she had privacy, and finding things for her to do for the rest of us. She enjoyed helping with the cooking, and quite often I'd hear her and Sara in the kitchen together, chatting about all sorts of things.

It was only a few days later though that Mum had a nasty fall. She'd obviously passed out again, and this time had broken her arm. They said they'd keep her in at the hospital, and so Sara and I headed up there for visiting time.

Mum was quite distracted and her thoughts seemed miles away. Then she turned to me and said, 'Marion, you know I was frightened of dying, well I just want to say that I'm not any more. I've had lots of dreams about it recently, and I've dreamt about my own mam and dad, and about your dad, and I kind of sense that they're waiting for me to join them.'

I was really taken aback. Mum was one of those solid, down-to-earth types and talking about dreams wasn't anything I'd heard her do before. It's the kind of thing she'd usually dismiss as nonsense. So I just nodded and waited to see what was going to happen next.

I think I'm ready to die now. I'm tired of being such a burden. My bones are old, and it's time they had a rest. You've been really good to me, looking after me, but it's not the same as being in my own home. I think there's another home waiting for me now and I'm just waiting for the angels to take me there.

That was quite a speech for Mum. But she was relaxed now, and seemed very peaceful. We talked a bit about things that we'd done in the past and Sara listened as her gran talked about how she felt after my dad died. And then it was the end of visiting time. When I said goodbye, I just knew it was the last time I'd see Mum alive. Don't ask me how, but I did. Our eyes met, and it was then I knew she felt the same way. We didn't say anything, just kept looking, and then she smiled and patted my hand.

After we left the ward I found myself walking towards the chapel. Sara said she'd wait for me outside, and so I was on my own when a nun who worked in the chaplaincy team came up to me and asked if

I'd like to talk. I said no, but asked if she'd mind praying for my mum because I just couldn't find the words. So she did, and as she prayed I cried. I had this picture in my mind of me handing over Mum to Jesus, and asking him to love her like I did. And then I realized that he already did, and that it was right for Mum to die now. She was ready.

Early next morning the phone rang. It was the hospital to say that Mum had died in her sleep. I wasn't surprised, and although I was still really upset, I knew that Mum would be happy. Later on I talked to Sister Maria about it, the nun at the hospital, and she said that though I was glad for Mum's sake it didn't mean that I couldn't mourn her.

That was good advice because I missed Mum like crazy. I kept going into her room expecting her to be there, and then I cleared out her old house and felt that there was so much of her I never knew. Yet every time I took flowers to her grave, I felt at one with the world and one with God. There really is a time to be born, and a time to die.

It's impossible to summarize a chapter about struggling to make sense of it all. But in not finding all the answers, and in struggling together through faith and love, the paradox is that we can come closer to God. We can see that suffering is not the opposite of love, but rather an integral and productive part of it. This is not to suggest, of course, that we should seek pain in our lives in order to grow. That would be macabre and masochistic. But living through pain is extremely important, even the bitter pain of the death of a partner. And in the aching pain and confusion and emptiness of our bereavement, and in the kindness and comfort of others, we find God, and the very author of love itself.

So let us value life, all of it. Life is a gift from God and as we laugh and cry, and love and argue, let us live it as fully as we can. We can't hoard it; we can't lock it in a safety deposit box. We never know when it may end. And on the days when the pain of loving caused by death feels too much to bear, we can draw courage from the knowledge that God shares it all with us. He mourns with us, he strengthens us, and he helps us to prepare for the day when we too will enter into the glory of the kingdom which may lie beyond this world. Then, maybe then, we will fully understand why we are born, and live, and die.

ORGANIZATIONS FOR THE BEREAVED

There are many organizations who offer support and a listening ear to people who are bereaved. It is not possible to include all of them here, because many are local initiatives which will need to be found through the local library, or the local Social Services Department or Citizen's Advice Bureau. The national organizations included below have information, a helpline, or local support groups.

COMPASSIONATE FRIENDS
53, North Street,
Bristol BS3 1EN
Telephone: (0117) 9539639
A self-help organization for parents whose child has died, at any age, and of any cause.

CRUSE BEREAVEMENT CARE
Cruse House,
126, Sheen Road,
Richmond,
Surrey TW9 1UR
Telephone: 0181-940 4818
Helpline (Mon–Fri, 9.30–5.00): 0181-332 7227
Offers counselling, advice, and social contact for the bereaved.

THE FOUNDATION FOR THE STUDY OF INFANT DEATHS
14, Malkin Street,
London SW1X 7DP
Telephone: 0171-235 0965
Offers support to bereaved parents, by letter, phone and support groups. Raises funds for research into cot deaths, and offers information.

NATIONAL ASSOCIATION OF BEREAVEMENT SERVICES
20, Norton Foldgate,
London E1 6DB
Telephone: 0171-247 0617
Helpline (Mon-Fri, 10.00-4.00): 0171-247 1080
Holds information on all types of bereavement support
throughout the country.

THE STILLBIRTH AND NEONATAL DEATH SOCIETY
(SANDS)
28, Portland Place,
London W1N 4DE
Telephone: 0171-436 5881
Offers telephone support, information and local support
groups.

GAY BEREAVEMENT PROJECT
Vaughan M. Williams Centre,
Colindale Hospital,
London NW9 5HG
Telephone: 0181-200 0511
Helpline: 0181-455 8894
Offers telephone support.

Appendix 2
BOOKS FOR FURTHER READING

This is by no means a conclusive list of books on bereavement. I have tried, though, to cover a range of experience, and different types of approach.

D. Winter, *What Happens After Death?*, Lion Pocketbook, 1991. ISBN 0 7459 2137 X

R. M. Youngson, *Grief. Rebuilding Your Life After Bereavement*, David and Charles Publishers, 1989. ISBN 0 7153 9160 7

A. Whitaker, ed. *All in the End is Harvest: An Anthology for Those who Grieve*, Darton, Longman and Todd in association with CRUSE, 1985. ISBN 0 232 51624 3

N. Kohner and A. Henley, *When a Baby Dies*, Pandora Press, 1995. ISBN 0 04 4405934-6

E. Kubler-Ross, *On Life After Death*, Celestial Arts, USA, 1992. ISBN 0890 87653

S. Key, *Freddie: A Diary of a Cot-Death*, Mandarin Paperbacks, 1991. ISBN 0 7493 0796 X

A. Lake, *Living With Grief*, Sheldon Press, 1984. ISBN 0 85969 426 7

P. Mullen, *Death Be Not Proud*, Fount Paperbacks, 1989. ISBN 0 00 627467 6

C. Murray Parkes, *Bereavement: Studies of Grief in Adult Life*, Routledge, 1996. ISBN 0 415 11033 5

H. Kushner, *When Bad Things Happen to Good People*, Schocken, NY, 1989. ISBN 0 805 24039 X

A DEATH IN THE FAMILY
Jean Richardson

Someone you love has died... what do you do first? How do you arrange the funeral? How long will the pain of grief last? How can you find hope for the future?

Jean Richardson's sympathetic guide is for anyone who has to deal with a death in the family. It explains how to prepare for bereavement and provides practical advice concerning the funeral, the will, and all the other details that must be dealt with. Even more important, it guides the reader through the emotional and spiritual aspects of bereavement, providing support for the darkest times and hope for the future.

ISBN 0 7459 2387 9

LIVING THROUGH GRIEF
Harold Bauman

'The crisis of grief comes to everyone sooner or later... There are things which we can know ahead of time to help us when we experience grief and to help us give understanding, comfort, and encouragement to bereaved friends.'

Harold Bauman writes for those suffering the emotional trauma of grief, especially following the death of someone close. He guides the reader through the different stages of grief which anyone coping with this loss can expect. And in this sensitive and helpful book, he also shares the special comfort and resources which a Christian faith offers at this crisis in life.

ISBN 0 7459 1617 1

LOSING A CHILD
Elaine Storkey

The loss of a child may happen in many different ways. But each lost child is precious. And behind each loss there is grief. How can we cope with the shock and the pain?

Where can we turn for help? Who will answer the 'whys' and 'if onlys'?

This is a helpful, positive book. It faces the pain; it also offers encouragement and hope.

ISBN 0 7459 1530 2

THE PATH OF PEACE
Norman Warren

For centuries Psalm 23 has brought peace, reassurance and hope to countless people.

This book explores the shepherd psalm afresh. Is there an answer to anxiety, loneliness and fear? And can we know the 'shepherd' for ourselves?

By best-selling author Norman Warren, this attractive, helpful book brings a message of hope and new life to the reader of today.

ISBN 0 7459 1370 9

WHAT HAPPENS AFTER DEATH?
David Winter

Can we know anything for sure about life beyond the grave?

What is heaven like?

Will there be a judgment?

David Winter explores the Bible's answers in a way that speaks clearly to those facing death or bereavement.

ISBN 0 7459 2137 X

WORDS OF COMFORT

Through the centuries the words of the Bible have been a source of faith and devotion, inspiration and peace of mind. They have brought hope and comfort to countless men and women down the ages.

In this book extracts from the Bible have been grouped around one main theme. The passages speak directly to the hopes and fears of people today, in the fresh and simple language of the Good News Bible. Full-colour photographs opposite each quotation reflect the thought and mood of the writers.

ISBN 0 7459 1969 3

EMMA SAYS GOODBYE
Carolyn Nystrom

Auntie Sue was full of fun. She was strong, too—strong enough to climb telegraph poles and mend wires. But not now. Now Auntie Sue was having tests and seeing the doctor and going to the hospital. She was too ill to work.

Emma was frightened. Maybe Auntie Sue wasn't going to get better... Emma began to feel angry. Why didn't God answer her prayers?

Coming to terms with the death of someone close is hard. But Emma and her family have time to work through their hurt. Carolyn Nystrom's gentle story explains what is happening to Auntie Sue as her illness progresses—and how Emma, her family and Auntie Sue herself react. It removes fears and offers comfort and hope.

ISBN 0 7459 1608 2

All Lion paperbacks are available from your local bookshop, or can be ordered direct from Lion Publishing. For a free catalogue, showing the complete list of titles available, please contact:

Customer Services Department
Lion Publishing plc
Peter's Way
Sandy Lane West
Oxford OX4 5HG

Tel: (01865) 747550
Fax: (01865) 715152